The Diaspora Student and Youth Front

A Cause that Matters in Your
Curriculum, Career, and Connection

David A. Mayom

The publisher wishes to acknowledge and thank Dr. Douglas H. Johnson for his invaluable help and support for Africa World Books and its mission of preserving and promoting African cultural and literary traditions and history. Dr. Johnson and fellow historians have been instrumental in ensuring that African people remain connected to their past and their identity. Africa World Books is proud to carry on this mission.

Cover design, typesetting and layout : Africa World Books

Table of Contents

Acknowledgement

I am grateful to the Almighty God for having reached this far. I am also immensely indebted to many people and entities who inspired and supported me. First and foremost, I dedicate this book to my family: father, mother, wife, and daughter. My late father, Solomon Mayom Apioth, taught students and administered schools for nearly 40 years. He was a teacher and father-figure to many war affected-children known as the Lost Boys of Sudan from the beginning until they left for the U.S., Australia, Canada, and other countries. Most of my inspiration and passion for choosing a career in academia comes from his long legacy of teaching and caring for the younger generations. My mother, Adhieu Marol Biar, is a wonderful mother who helped me survive the tumultuous war-era in the then Sudan when I was a child. Although I was one of the youngest *Jesh Amer*, an Arabic term for the Lost Boys of Sudan, I still had to split my stay between Jesh Amer camp and my parents' home. This gave me an advantage over most boys who did not have parents in Ethiopia and Kenya. On the other hand, I highly appreciate my young family, my wife (Akuch Agot Alier) and my daughter (Alakiir Ayual Mayom) whose patience helped me accomplish the writing of this book.

Furthermore, I am indebted to the United Nation (U.N.) agencies, the U.S. government and its people. As part of the Lost Boys of Sudan, without basic needs support from the U.N., our tragic journey characterized by a high death rate and suffering would not have been possible. Similarly, I am thankful to the U.S. government for taking us in at a critical stage of human and intellectual growth. When I was about to finish my high school education in Kenya, I was given an opportunity to resettle in the U.S. along with 3,400 other boys and a few girls in the early 2000s. I took the chance and obtained an American education from two great universities.

On the home front, I am also indebted to the people who fought and sacrificed to liberate the South Sudanese people. For these heroes and heroines, many paid the ultimate sacrifice, and others live with eternal bullet scars. This is our greatest generation. Without this generation, we would not have a country called South Sudan that we are proud of and feel a sense of belonging to today.

Professionally, I am very thankful to my South Sudan STEM Initiative (SSSTEM) team: the leadership board made up of Dr.

Amanda Nguyen, Spencer MacColl, Pierre Kolowe, and Simon Deng, and the advisory board members, Dr. Jacob Dut Chol, and Dr. James Alic Garang. These remarkable colleagues and friends believed in my founding vision and mission of promoting science, technology, engineering, and mathematics (STEM) education in South Sudan. We worked together for three years until May 2019 when SSSTEM launched and opened its first solar-powered computer lab at Dr. John Garang Secondary School, Twic East County, Jonglei State, South Sudan. This was one of the first computer labs in South Sudan public schools. Since then, SSSTEM has also provided various educational resources and promoted academic programs across the country. Currently, SSSTEM is set to open a second computer lab in Mongalla Displaced Camp, Central Equatoria State.

Last but not least, I am grateful for the invaluable inputs from two colleagues: Dr. Daniel Akech Thiong and Engr. Thon Kuany Arok who painstakingly read the drafts and provided insightful inputs and edits that have enriched this book.

Foreword

I was introduced to David Mayom in 2015 via a friend and co-author who recommended him to support a study examining the impacts of Kakuma refugee camp in northern Kenya on the host population. At the time, what I knew was that he came with a very strong endorsement, and that he had spent at least part of his youth in Kakuma, which made him a great fit for the job. Little did I know how lucky I was! The project involved interviewing host nationals as well as refugees from a number of different countries within the camp. The entire enterprise was fraught with logistical challenges and delays, including some very delicate situations around the management of the team within the camp. Without David's grace, diplomacy, efficacy, and excellent humor we may not have succeeded at all. This work resulted in a World Bank Report that has been downloaded over 4,000 times, and a number of academic papers. If it has also resulted in a broader understanding of the complexity and importance of interactions between displaced people and the communities where they live, then this is in no small part due to David's work.

Since 2015, I have had the great pleasure of finding surprise updates in my inbox detailing his latest activities. The messages have never failed to impress – lecturer at Upper Nile University, motivational speaker in California, founder of an NGO touching the lives of the people in his homeland, and then, father. I was delighted to recently open up the latest one of these messages: "I have just finished writing a book…" As if it were the easiest and most natural thing in the world! This understated and joyful embrace of new experience is the essence of all of the communications that I have received from David. As you will soon discover in this book, he has a knack for making things which seem daunting entirely doable. There is no one more qualified than David to reflect on the challenges, practical considerations, and most importantly, the transformative possibilities of diaspora children connecting to their home country, and for youth from everywhere benefitting from service-oriented study, work, and travel.

As we reach the middle of 2022, feeling as though we might finally be emerging from two years of isolation and trauma induced by the coronavirus pandemic, the message of this book feels like a healing salve. The book is ostensibly directed at diaspora families who may have not been permitted to go back to their home countries during these recent years, but it is also directed at all of us. It also reminds us our connections to each other and the range of ways, big and small, in which we can serve others. David offers clear and practical advice for how families from all kinds of backgrounds can orient their work, study, and travel towards the purpose of supporting and connecting with communities across the globe, whether they can afford a year of dedicating volunteering abroad, an hour a week on Zoom, or the collection of pencils, pens, and notebooks in Los Angeles to send to a school in Kenya. As he wisely reminds us, this connection is a two-way street: those that are "giving" benefit as much and sometimes more than those who "receive" the training or school supplies.

Most importantly, this book reminds us that we are connected to the present and the future through our children, and that raising them with an understanding of our interconnectedness is essential to building a future where we solve problems as a society, not as individuals fighting for the preservation of our personal piece of the pie.

I hope that as you read through these pages you experience the same moments of inspiration, understanding, and elevation of your sense of purpose that I have.

Jennifer Alix-Garcia
Professor of Applied Economics
Oregon State University

Preface

Although the book specifies "Diaspora" in the title of the book, that does not preclude any student and youth who is not a diaspora person. The word is used in the sense of giving diaspora students and youths more roles since they have two roots - one in their countries of origin and another in their adopted countries. However, any global-minded student with passion and interest in volunteering causes can read and apply the concepts in this book.

The word "Front" in the title has a nationalist and globalist connotation for a volunteering cause. If you are a nationalist whose country of origin is disadvantaged in terms of socio-economic progress, you would prioritize the fight for social progress of that country. An example is when a diaspora student travels to volunteer at a hospital, school, or orphanage in their country of origin as their contribution toward the development. If you are a globalist from a developed country, you would fight against the global inequalities wherever you are, or travel to an oversea developing country to volunteer in any way necessary.

The book is mainly meant for high school, undergraduate, and graduate students. However, an advanced and well-prepared middle school student can also benefit from reading the book. The words "student" and "youth" may sound like synonyms to some readers, but they are different in the context of this book. While most students are youth, many youths are not students, and so the need for both in the usage. As for the definition of "youth," the book refers to many developing countries that define youth as young people between 14 to 35 years old.

I do not use the word, "Matter" found in the subtitle in a light sense. The word is used to emphasize the very importance of the cause, just like in the "Black Lives Matter" movement. In this book's context, the cause matters both to the recipient and the provider of the service. For example, a volunteering action you take may change someone's life forever, whether it is an idea, a service, or a material support. On the other hand, you will have a better perspective and sense of purpose in life.

Even though the book is primarily meant for students and youths, it is also necessary that a parent read it. This way, the parent can provide guidance and support to their child with full understanding of the program and activity. At the minimum, it is highly recommended that a parent read the last chapter, titled, "Notes to Parents."

On the other hand, a student or youth is not required to read this Chapter V, but is welcome to do so, as it provides more emphasis.

As a disclaimer, the book is neither about child development programs nor legal parenting advice. The book is purely based on existing academic, career-related, volunteering, and impact-oriented programs that a diaspora student and youth can exploit for the benefit of their country and continent of origin.

David A. Mayom

Chapter 1

From the African Savannah to Silicon Valley:
A Tragic Journey Made Possible by Hope

From Wanglei, Southern Sudan
to Pinyudo Refugee Camp, Ethiopia

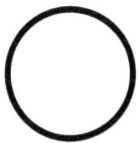

On a typical day in the beautiful and pristine African savannah of the Jonglei state of Sudan, imagine little Dinka boys herding cows and playing in the sunny late morning. I was one of these boys. Each morning after the milking of the cows was done by the women, several of us would gather our cattle for grazing in the nearby rich pasture areas. While the cattle were grazing majestically in the lush greenland, we would play different fun games, such as hide and seek, and wrestling.

Meanwhile, able-bodied adult men from my village and other parts of the country were mobilizing for war. The cattle pastoralists, farmers, secondary and university students, and civil servants from Southern and Central Sudan were taking up arms to fight against the political, ethnic, and religious oppression from the Arab-dominated government in Khartoum. The new recruits flocked to the military training camps in Ethiopia. They joined the rebel army, the Sudan People's Liberation Army/Sudan People's Liberation Movement (SPLA/SPLM) formed on June 8th, 1983. They were led by the then army colonel, Dr. John Garang de Mabior.

By 1987, the civil war had reached deep into the villages of the southern part of the country. My village was located next to the court township of Wanglei, the present day Twic East County, Jonglei State, South Sudan. Here, the Sudanese army and air force started bombing civilians indiscriminately, leading to the killing of many civilians and destruction of properties. Men and boys from these southern villages were particular targets for killing as they were suspected of actively supporting the SPLA/SPLM.

In November 1987, in an effort to save the boys, later known as the Lost Boys of Sudan, they were gathered by clan chiefs and a few SPLA soldiers for a trek to the neighboring country of Ethiopia. There were over 20,000 boys, mostly from the southern villages. Due to my young age, I was about six years at the time, I couldn't go along with the rest of the boys. Fortunately, a couple of months later, my mother, siblings and I left for Ethiopia by a vehicle arranged by one of my relatives. My father was on an SPLA/SPLM military assignment.

Our trip to Ethiopia was smooth for two days until the vehicle got stuck while crossing the Ajuara River, about 40 miles west of Pochalla, the last town before entering Ethiopia. When it was clear it would take a long time before the vehicle was dug out, we, the passengers, were asked by the army captain in charge of the trip to walk by foot to Pochalla. For a young boy of my age, walking bare-footed in muddy and thorny paths for a long distance was a terrible experience. About a day later, the vehicle finally made it to Pochalla late in the morning. The next day, the vehicle took off for Pinyudo refugee camp, Ethiopia, and arrived a few hours later.

The scenes in the camp were that of a bush being cleared to erect makeshift shelters. The Lost Boys could be seen everywhere making improvised thatch huts. There were a few established huts made of corrugated iron sheets. My family proceeded and put up with a relative in one of the adult community blocks. A few months later, my father, who was the SPLA/SPLM head librarian in Bilpam, Ethiopia, was tasked by the leadership to come to Pinyudo as one of the teachers for the Lost Boys. My father, commonly known as Ustaz Mayom, *ustaz* is an Arabic word for a teacher, arrived in Pinyudo in April 1988. He immediately took the family and settled us in the community section of the camp known as block nine before embark-ing on his teaching, caring, and mentoring role of the Lost Boys.

The settlements for the Jesh Amer were initially divided into twelve groups each with respective school areas. Ustaz Mayom was initially assigned to group and school number seven. About a year later, he was switched to group and school number ten where he stayed for the rest time in Pinyudo. As one of the military trained teachers, my father would regularly take the boys deep into nearby tribal territories called Gok Anyuak and Pan de John Umot acting as the boys' armed security guard. These were the areas where the boys would get building materials, such as logs and grasses for huts and fences.

When the schools opened in May 1988, due to my tender age, I was enrolled in school number one while I stayed with my parents at the block nine community section of the camp.

But I was regularly required by my father to participate in Jesh Amer activities to gain first-hand experience and *zopkurop*, an Arabic word that loosely translated as a military discipline. To do this, my father required me to go and stay in the Jesh Amer quarters for months in a row to get an experience of what the other boys were going through, a life of misery and survival. One of my tough experiences was the Jesh Amer three-month military training, in 1989, in a place called Markus, some ten miles away from the camp. My father told me, and my elder brother, that we must go with the rest of the boys for military training. Otherwise, we would not learn zopkurop. For this reason, I went to Markus in the second batch. The regimented military actions were harsh. I can still remember, very vividly, some of the routine activities, such as waking up at three a.m. to go and sing military motivational songs. In the afternoon, we would go to the bush to practice maneuvers like crawling flat on the chest, running and dropping into a defensive crouch, and zig-zagging around trees to imitate battlefield tactical maneuvers. The military training was done to familiarize the boys with the revolutionary ideals and to be readied for combat, if called upon, which was a common practice for the boys in their mid-teenage years.

On the educational front, the SPLA/SPLM was very emphatic

RADDA BARNEN
ADDIS ABEBA FIELD OFFICE

PIGNUDO REFUGEE CHILDREN'S PROJECT
DOCUMENTATION OF UNACCOMPAIED MINORS

SOCIAL HISTORY
AND ASSESSMENT

IDENTIFICATION

1. NAME	FATHER'S NAME	GRAND FATHER'S NAME	2-4
AYUAL	MAYOM	APIOTH	CARD NUMBER

2. OTHER NAME :—

CARD NUMBER: C O 7 6 9

2-2 CURRENT ADDRESS

SITE PIGNUDO   GROUP 1   SUB GROUP 5

2-3 DATE OF ARRIVAL   DAY ____ MONTH 11 YEAR 87

3 SEX   1. MALE ☑   2 FEMALE ☐

3-1 YEAR OF BIRTH   83

3-2 ETHNIC GROUP   DINKA

3-3 CLAN   PAN – APIDIN

3-4 LANGUAGE   A) MOTHER TONGUE DINKA   B) OTHER(S) NONE

3-5 RELIGION   1 CHRISTIAN ☐   3 ANIMIST ☑   2 MOSLEM ☐   4 OTHER ☐

3-6 HIGHEST GRADE COMPLETED   NONE

My first personal information (in
Dinka's full name) from Radda Barnen.
Radda Barnen (1988). Pignudo Refugee Children's Project Documentation
of Unaccompanied Minors: Social History and Assesment. Lost Boys
Center For Leadership Development. https://lostboysreunited.com/

about the boys and few girls that they were getting education while simultaneously participating in other revolutionary activities. Case in point, the Lost Boys composed one of the famous songs, *amuk galam ne chin cueech ku dhang ne chin cam,* a mixture of Dinka and Arabic words that means the SPLA/SPLM leadership expected the boys to juggle the pen on the right hand and the gun on the left hand. This was to show the importance of education to the revolution.

The first schools were in the open spaces under the trees. There were no stationery, such as pens, exercise books or teaching materials, like chalks, blackboards, and textbooks. Without these resources, the alternative was to use the ground as a notebook, a finger on the ground as a pen, and the teacher forced to do a one-on-one check to make sure the students were getting the lessons. Fortunately, a few months later, the United Nations International Children's Emergency Fund (UNICEF) came in with stationery and teaching materials. Although there was still a shortage of educational resources, sharing the little that was given was quite a relief. The struggle to survive and inadequate primary education continued the rest of the time in Ethiopia, until May 1991, when the Lost Boys were forced out of Ethiopia.

The Escape From Pinyudo to Pochalla

The collapse of the Union of Soviet Socialist Republics (U.S.S.R.) in 1991 and the existing cold war dynamics between the world super-powers reverberated in Africa and beyond. The Derg regime, under Mengistu Haile Mariam, in Ethiopia was allied to the Socialist Bloc.

Therefore, with the collapse of the U.S.S.R., the Derg regime was toppled by the rebel groups, namely the Tigray People Liberation Front (TPLF) and Eritrea People Liberation Front (EPLF) supported by the western bloc. The new TPLF regime, under Meles Zenawi, pushed the refugees out of Pinyudo camp. We had no other route but to return to Pochalla, Southern Sudan. The walk from the camp to Pochalla, on foot, took days. It was the second time I had to walk a very long distance.

Even more traumatic was crossing the Gilo River. Due to the political differences and earlier battle encounter between the Ethiopian rebels and SPLA/SPLM, the Ethiopian rebels came and attacked the thousands of Southern Sudanese refugees just before crossing the Gilo River. The situation became very chaotic and deadly. There were a very few boats to ferry people to the other side. Many people attempted to cross by swimming but drowned because they did not know how to swim. Others were killed before and during the crossing of the river. Several thousand people died during this attack. My family narrowly made it to the other side of the river less than an hour before the attack.

Those of us who made it to Pochalla had to deal with the challenge of meeting the bare minimum of basic needs. Pochalla was a garrison town with only a few permanent structures. We had to make ourselves a makeshift shelter in the allotted bushy areas and find food anywhere we could. We struggled like this for three months before the United Nations High Commissioner for Refugees (UNHCR) got in with supplies of basic necessities.

The Flight from Pocholla to Kakuma Refugee Camp, Northern Kenya

Before the end of seven months, Pochalla was attacked and overrun by the Sudan government soldiers. At the time of attack, the Lost Boys had already left Pochalla a few weeks earlier after receiving intelligence about the pending assault on the town. My family and many other people who were residing in the community quarters did not leave on time, and had to face the brunt of the enemy onslaught. Government soldiers began their attack just across the main river before entering Pochalla. Coincidentally, my younger brother and I were swimming and playing in the same river at the moment of the attack. We had to run as fast as our legs could carry us toward our home, not knowing whether we would reach our house due to the barrage of bullets flying all over. Upon arriving home, we found our mother and siblings hiding in a ditch overwhelmed by tears. They thought we had died. Our father just made it from where he had been spending time with a relative.

Given the chaos and confusion generated by the attack, the residents of Pochalla town were forced to go in two general directions. One group headed toward The SPLA/SPLM garrison at Boma, Jonglei state. This was the same route taken by the Lost Boys weeks earlier. The second group headed in the direction of Ukello, a small garrison town within Jonglei state. My father decided to take our family toward Ukello due to the presence of the enemy on the path of the Boma route. While on the escape route, the attacking force intensified artillery shelling. In the process, many were killed, others injured, and some experienced episodes of deafness due to the sound of the guns. After two gloomy days, our family and everyone on this route arrived in Ukello.

Meanwhile, the SPLA/SPLM split into two factions due to political and power struggles. Under Dr. John Garang de Mabior, the mainstream SPLA-Torit, based in Torit, was mostly composed of soldiers from the Dinka and other tribes of Sudan. The break-away, SPLA-Nasir, based in Nasir, under Dr. Riek Machar Teny, was mainly made up of soldiers from the Nuer and Shilluk tribes. It was a very tragic split that led to the death of tens of thousands of people on both sides.

As a garrison town, Ukello was a potential enemy target. A few weeks after arrival, a momentous decision had to be made by the displaced persons. Since most of the people in Ukello were of the Dinka tribe, the options were to go back to their ancestral lands in Upper Nile and Bahr el Ghazal region or follow the route taken by the Lost Boys toward the Equatoria region. With the path heading to Equatoria littered with enemy soldiers and hostile ethnic groups, most people decided to go to their homes within Upper Nile and Bahr el Ghazal. However, my father, being one of the Lost Boys' teachers, took a chance to follow the Equatorian path of the Lost Boys. Fortunately, the commander of the Ukello SPLA/SPLM soldiers who happened to be a former high schoolmate of my father found a spot for my family in one of the army vehicles heading to Boma. The family made it to Boma, and caught another U.N. truck heading to Kapoeta, Eastern Equatoria state. After spending two weeks in Kapoeta, my family got into another U.N. truck heading to Narus, a town near the Sudan-Kenya border, where the Lost Boys had been settled weeks earlier. Upon arriving in Narus, my father took up his task as one of the caretaker teachers in one of the Lost Boys' groups while the rest of my family members were settled in the community section.

A few weeks later, the SPLA/SPLM strategic garrison town of Kapoeta was captured by the government troops who were expected to proceed to Narus where the Lost Boys and civilians were settled. Knowing the enemy's intention was to kill the Lost Boys and civilians indiscriminately, in June 1992, the SPLA/SPLM decided to move the Lost Boys and civilians to Kakuma refugee camp, Kenya. But we first had to walk for a day to the Kenyan border town of Lokichogio, and wait there for weeks before being finally transported to Kakuma.

Like previous refugee and displaced person camps, Kakuma was a bushy place; a dusty, hot, and semi-arid region of the Turkana people, a Nilotic ethnic group of East Africa. Kakuma became our home for the next ten years. It was a place characterized by harsh conditions, where people often ate once a day or went without food due to the lack of it. Similar to the previous camps, Kakuma was split into the Lost Boys groups and adult-family groups. My family settled in the adult-family group number forty nine. While my father stayed with us most of the time, he was also assigned to teach and care for the Lost Boys in group number seven when schooling started early in 1993.

I was enrolled in school in 1993, picking up in third grade, where I left off schooling in Pinyudo. I began at Cush Primary School as a low-performing student in terms of grades, ranking around the bottom third of my class every term. At this time, I mostly liked to spend a vast amount of my time playing soccer, going to church for Sunday school dancing, and enjoying other children's games. Interestingly, the turning point for me, performance wise, was when my father came up with an idea for the prize for the best student, as a way to promote academic competition among my siblings and cousins. The prize would only go to anyone who ranked number one in their class, as the Kenyan grading system was rank-based. At first, the merit prize would go to my cousin, who also happened to be my classmate, who ranked first in class almost every term. The content of the award usually varied each term, ranging from new clothes and shoes to highly envied soccer balls to funny picture books. Additionally, there were constant praises for the awardee from relatives and peers. The prizes and praises were tantalizing, and I was encouraged to aim for them. I redoubled my study time and drastically reduced the time for other activities to focus on studying. The effort paid off as I kept on rising in my class.

Fast forward to the first term of fifth grade in 1995, I became the top student in our class, pushing my cousin to the second position. Once I tasted the value and perks of the prize, I would maintain the top position for the rest of the year. To make it more exciting, my father made me his teaching assistant (TA) for grading and recording student exam papers, for multiple choices, fill-in-the blanks, and true or false kinds of questions. In 1996, feeling a little invincible, I decided to skip sixth grade, avoiding sixth grade altogether, and moving to seventh grade. I had to leave Cush for Buma Primary School since my current school did not allow skipping a class.

Although I did not lead my new class in the seventh grade, I managed to study hard and stay as one of the top five students for the next two years. I eventually succeeded in leading my class in the Kenya Certificate of Primary Education (KCPE) examination in 1997. Fortunately, in 1998, I won the Episcopal Church scholarship to study in Katilu Boys Secondary School, located in the same district. In high school, I also did very well, performance wise. I remained there until January 2001 when I had to leave for resettlement in the United States. Looking back, I credited my father's prize with my success in primary school and all the subsequent academic achievements.

The Journey to the United States of America

In the late 1990s, the U.S. government came up with the program to resettle several thousand of the Lost Boys to the United States. Although the resettlement was essentially a humanitarian gesture, it was also a strategic U.S. foreign policy with economic interests. By bringing the Lost Boys to the United States, they were expected to get an American education and learn Western values, which they could eventually take back to Sudan. In the process creating an American ally in the region. Former U.S. President, George Bush, confirmed this while addressing the Lost Boys in Dallas, Texas, in 2016, when he said the Lost Boys would be the best "ambassadors" of American and universal values when they finally returned to their homeland. On the economic interest, most of the Lost Boys were young adults who got jobs and became self-reliant, thus their signif-icant contributions to America's economy.

In November 2000, the first batch of the Lost Boys and a few girls arrived in the U.S. By late 2001, most of the nearly 3,400 boys had reached the U.S. and resettled across the major cities. Those who were adults by age, 18 years old and up, had to live independently whereas those who were 17 years old and younger had to live with foster parents. My younger brother and I arrived in Seattle, Washington, on January 31, 2001, as part of the group sponsored by the United States Conference of Catholic Bishops (USCCB). My brother, who was 16 years old at the time, was placed with a foster family. I was aged 19 years old, and was given a place in an exclusive apartment building with a group of other boys. Catholic nuns previously occupied the apartment complex before it was transferred to us. Since all the new residents of the building were Lost Boys, we renamed it *Payam House*, the word for an administrative unit in Southern Sudan. The sponsor, USCCB, paid three months of our living expenses, after which we were expected to find jobs, move out of the complex, and start being self-reliant.

I searched and applied extensively for a job. I found my first job in April 2001 as a warehouse worker in a tourist souvenir warehouse. I would pull out souvenirs, print pricing labels, pack and prepare the boxes for shipping to various stores. I also drove a forklift to receive and store warehouse goods. Having a job was exciting and fun for me. Getting a paycheck and sending back money to relatives in Africa was something almost every Lost Boy longed for, and felt obligated to do.

Since I left Kenya while in twelfth grade, but before completing my high school diploma, I had to complete my high school diploma equivalence, the General Educational Development (GED), before I could begin college. I studied and completed my GED in December 2001, and started taking classes at Seattle Central Community College in the Spring Quarter 2002. I had to contend with full time work and school. It quickly got harder to find sufficient time to sleep and relax on the weekdays since I was still using public transportation. Sometimes, I would sleepover at a friend's place when I had late night classes. Nevertheless, I kept pressing on.

In 2004, when I was set to transfer my credits to the university, I took a leave from school to work two jobs in order to solve a family issue that needed my immediate financial support. I came back to school in January 2006, and transferred to Washington State University. I graduated in May 2008 with a Bachelor of Arts in Economics.

I had a plan to work in the financial industry, but my graduation precisely coincided with the 2007-2009 global financial crisis, also known as the Great Recession, when the U.S. was losing about 216,000 jobs every month. It was the worst economic downturn since the Great Depression that began in 1929 and ended ten years later. Consequently, I worked as a staff accountant and commercial driver for Veolia Transportation Company before returning to graduate school in 2012 at the University of San Francisco. I studied and graduated with a Master of Science in International and Development Economics in May 2015.

Upon graduation, I immediately started my career at the World Bank Group as a research consultant in Kenya. In 2016, I left this job and returned to Juba, the capital of South Sudan, becoming an economics lecturer at Upper Nile University. While still teaching at the university, during the holidays, I would occasionally go to the countryside to visit my family and assess the state of primary and secondary school education. Shockingly, I found the condition of education was in a deplorable state. I found that many primary school students were taught under the trees and mud hut structures with perforated roofs that forced students to go home when it started raining. There were very few secondary students relative to the students' population. There was a very poor quality of education; most of the teachers were untrained, and many others were just waiting for the greener pastures. There were no adequate learning facilities such as libraries, science labs, and computer labs. The student enrolment rate was very low. According to UNICEF, in 2017, South Sudan had the lowest enrolment rate (over 70% unenrolled) of school-age children among the war-affected countries.

In 2018, troubled by this desolated condition of education in South Sudan, I returned to California, to run a non-profit organization, the South Sudan Science, Technology, Engineering, and Mathematics Initiative (SSSTEM), that I co-founded two years earlier. The mission of SSSTEM is to reinforce STEM education by providing related resources to disadvantaged schools across South Sudan. The primary way through which SSSTEM does this is by equipping school facilities with computers loaded with learning programs and applications. Essentially, providing a computer lab that serves as a technology center and digital library. The vision is to promote socio-economic advancement by preparing young people for the technical jobs of the 21st century.

To do this, my team and I opened our first solar-powered computer lab in May 2019, in Twic East County, Jonglei State, South Sudan. It was one of the first computer labs in a public school in the county.

With the computer lab powered by solar panel light, the students can use the facility at night to study and do homework. Due to all these cumulative effects, the lab was reported to have been very helpful in students' success in their term and national exams. Although the lab equipment and parts were recently disassembled due to the threat of flood, SSSTEM plans to reinstall them and replicate this lab across the country. Besides a computer lab, SSSTEM has other programs such as awarding laptops to the best students of the South Sudan Certificate of Primary Education (SSCPE).

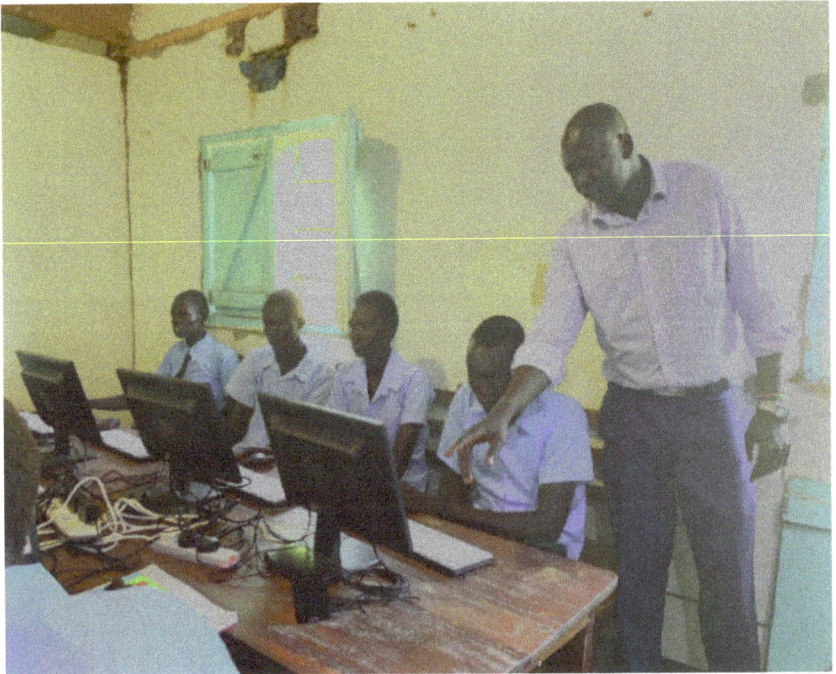

Here, I am guiding a student at the newly launched computer lab at Dr. John Garang Secondary School, Twic East County, Jonglei State, May 2019.

Another critical SSSTEM program, relevant to this book, is the facilitation of the diaspora student and youth volunteering activities in South Sudan. Based on various criteria, SSSTEM has established a number of primary and secondary schools and hospitals where a student or youth can choose to volunteer. For instance, a diaspora student can choose from this list of schools where to teach, tutor, and mentor during their holidays. They can work with the SSSTEM coordinator on the ground for a smooth experience. This is one of the main themes of this book.

PART I

Overseas Activities and Programs

Chapter 2

Magic Weeks of Fun, Volunteering, Learning, and Connecting

"Ask not what your country can do for you, ask what you can do for your country."

- Former U.S. President, John F. Kennedy

I n the context of this book, I use the definition of diaspora as persons or a group of people who live outside their homeland due to conflictual, economic, political, or religious reasons. A diaspora person may live comfortably in the country of their residence but identify more with their ancestral land. They may have an urge of patriotism that manifests in the form of financial support to relatives and developmental programs in their country of origin. For the most part, they also consider their children as part of the diaspora.

There are tens of millions of diaspora people worldwide. The largest diaspora groups are Indians, Chinese, and Mexicans who are away from their homelands mainly due to economic reasons. There are also Tibetans who are away from their ancestral land due to religious oppression. Lastly, there are Ethiopians, Jews, Vietnamese, Syrians, South Sudanese, Somalis, and other groups who left their homelands due to conflict. Each of these diaspora groups has a generation distinguished by a specific event and that becomes the history and legacy of that particular generation. Many of them long for the day they will return to their homeland and become part of the socio-economic progress.

However, there could also be a growing sense that their vibrant and productive age for fully contributing to the building of their nations is elapsing. They might need to prepare to pass on the mantle to the next generation, which happens to be their children, whom I called the seeds of the seeds. Figuratively, the parents are thought of as the original seeds, most of which did not reach harvest due to flood or pest. The few crops that survived the disaster get harvested and produced seeds for the next harvest and production. In the human context, if the parents did not have the opportunity to accomplish their generational duty, such as the Lost Boys, due to the instability caused by civil war and poor governance, their children get to take over that role when the time is ripe. The book's central theme is the connection of any diaspora student and youth, the seeds of seeds, to their ancestral land through various impact-oriented activities. This is their generational call and cause.

The original seed generation, the parents, might have been the generation that sacrificed so much before they found themselves in the diaspora. They might have fled ethnic and social violence. They might have left due to religious persecution. They could have fled due to economic hardship. Others gave up their childhood and fought in the battlefields with all their might. Fortunately, their children's generation did not have to go through the physical, emotional, and mental torture they went through. However, their children, the youth, have a different role they can play in humanitarian and impact related causes. Understandably, students and youths do not have many resources to carry out charity work. But they can work with what they have, as this has always been the idea of philanthropy. That is, people contributing whatever resources they have, whether money or time, to make the world a better place.

If you are a high school or university student, you can help change the world by imparting skills to fellow disadvantaged students. You can go back to your country of origin or any underdeveloped country to teach fellow underprivileged students or serve in other charitable ways. There are several ways to go overseas and volunteer: volunteering while on a study abroad program, taking a trip for a volunteering mission, and volunteering while on a long vacation with a family. For example, if you are equipped with technical and vocational skills, you can go to an under-developed country and offer free training at an established school. Furthermore, a financially stable youth endowed with capital resources can explore investment options from a myriad of opportunities in these developing countries. All of these are your generational causes.

There are several important reasons and benefits to volunteering as a student and youth. Besides connecting to your roots, it provides a greater sense of purpose to serve humanity; it is a remarkable legacy to serve a cause greater than yourself. More importantly, it makes your career resume and academic application stronger for any future opportunity. Whether applying for a job at a reputable global-focused company or a university admission, they will appreciate and admire someone who cares about impact-related causes. For these reasons, many colleges recommend international study and volunteering experience to their students. As a testimony, University of Adelaide says "98% of our returned students would recommend overseas study to their friends!" The following sections will explore many of these causes and experiences in detail.

An Overview: Overseas Causes

"Only a life lived for others is a life worthwhile."

- Physicist and humanitarian, Albert Einstein.

When Einstein, one of the world's greatest scientists, uttered this phrase, he said it with absolute certainty and objectivity, like any other scientific theory for which he had provided a proof. Essentially, he means service to others provides a sense of purpose and fulfillment in life, helps change the world as you make a mark no matter how small, and advances your career and academic development. The sense of purpose is also why many billionaires and millionaires who want to change the world ultimately donate much of their wealth to charities and good causes rather than distributing it among their heirs and friends. This is why many former presidents and other leaders dedicate their retirement years to causes benefiting underprivileged people. Now, imagine starting as a youth, with your contribution, the sky could be the limit for personal development, and change you could make to humanity.

In order to connect and learn your cultures, you likely attend your community gatherings and partake in cultural dances, church singing and dancing, wrestling activities, or listening to speeches. These local community activities are transformational and encouraged for young diasporans. However, in the end, if they are the only things you do to connect and learn your cultures then you are more like an athlete who only practices but never competes in the actual tournament. It will be like living in a bubble. As a diaspora youth, the following are many practical channels to experience your heritage first hand at home and in the region, as well as the chance to volunteer. Some are academic-related activities that may offer volunteer services within or outside the learning institution. Others are non-academic but career-related activities provided by non-governmental organiza-tions (NGOs), governments, and private entities. Lastly, others are self-designed projects that serve the needy people.

Overseas Academic-Related Activities for College and High School Students

As a college or high school student, you have several opportunities to travel overseas as part of your academic requirements. If possible, you can customize your trip to your country of origin. Contact your school international program and they will navigate you through the process of financial support and related requirements. Generally, the following opportunities are available in many schools as part of the international programs.

I. Foreign Exchange Study

This is a program in which a student travels to another country to study in a partner school or organization for a particular period. Apart from fulfilling academic requirements, the exchange program provides a student an opportunity to provide community service, experience different cultures, learn language, enhance career perspectives, and explore the country. For instance, if a student from a Western country wants to take a course related to African studies, development economics, or tropical diseases. It is practical to take this course as an exchange in an African or a South American country. This can make you more of a global-oriented citizen, thus, readying yourself to tackle some of the pressing global issues of modern times.

While on foreign exchange and study abroad program, a student may live in a hostel, student dormitory, student lodging, or with a host family or relative. The funding may be through a grant, scholarship, loan, or out of the student's own pocket.

There are two types of exchange programs: a short-term and long-term program. A short-term exchange may last from a few days to several months. It is mostly meant for a student to experience and understand other people's cultures, languages, and histories. It is also a great opportunity for adventure and volunteering activities.

A short-term exchange is typically arranged by governments, non-governmental organizations (NGOs), and non-profit organizations (NPOs). On the other hand, a long-term exchange takes two academic terms to a year. A long-term exchange program is intended to provide a more immersive exposure to the participants through studies, host family interactions, community service, and traveling for adventure. A long-term exchange offers a student the time and opportunity to volunteer. Depending on the partner school or organization, students may be allowed to volunteer internally or externally. For instance, a partner NGO may take exchange students to volunteer in the construction site of a community school within the town. Internally, a host school may offer volunteer opportunities, such as tutoring, peer mentoring, and others.

The cost for both short-term and long-term exchange varies depending on various factors, including, but not limited to, program type, length of time, host country, and school status. Some programs offer scholarships, grants, or loans to fund your study. For this information, check with your home school and overseas exchange school. Further, each exchange study program has a set of application requirements both from the home school and host school or organization. Requirements may include age limit, visa type, application fees, grade performance, interviews, letters of recommendation, and other institutional requirements. Once you arrive at the host school, there will be some safety restrictions. Examples are places you are not allowed to travel to, time of the day you cannot go out, and driving restrictions. Contact your school's international program for specific information on foreign exchange programs.

II. Study Abroad Program

When a college student chooses a study abroad program for a semester or a year, they opt for a more independent path of learning. A study abroad application and related information, such as financial assistance, are found through a host institution's office and website. In other words, there is no formal agreement between a student's home school and the overseas school. Unlike an exchange student, a study abroad student is not enrolled in their home school while studying overseas. Therefore, a study abroad student directly pays tuition and associated fees to a host school.

Due to the lack of an official agreement between a student's home school and the overseas school, the credit may or may not apply towards your degree. Hence, if you want your study abroad credits to apply toward your degree, check with your home school before committing. In addition, check with your home school for other helpful tips, such as the experiences of previous study abroad students, recommendations, and safety information.

Despite the differences between a foreign exchange and study abroad program, the benefits a student garners from both are, in most cases, very similar. From cultural exposure and language learning to career perspectives to community service, the advantages and experiences are identical. The difference is that an exchange program is pre-arranged and guided by a home school, whereas study abroad program gives a student leeway to choose any country and school based on their interest and other lifetime plans.

III. Research and Science Fair

Many undergraduate and graduate degree programs have opportunities for research in overseas countries as part of academic degree requirements. If you take this option and decide to visit a developing country, this can be a great chance to make an impact. If your research topic is in an impact-oriented study area, your research could transform the lives of poor people in that country and beyond. Topics abound in these areas, such as crop diseases and pests, human tropical diseases, technology for clean drinking water, cheaper engineering systems for lighting and communication, social investment, and many others.

For example, during my graduate studies at the University of San Francisco, I went to Kigali, Rwanda, for research as part of my master's coursework requirement. In my three-month data collection process, I worked with officials of the Rwanda Development Board (RBD) and The National Bank of Rwanda. I successfully collected my data on foreign direct investment (FDI) and conducted in-person case study interviews with the officials of these two institutions. In the end, I produced a data-based thesis titled, *"The Impact of Foreign Direct Investment on Labor Market Measures: Evidence From Sub-Saharan Africa."* The thesis has been published online and available for free download at the University of San Francisco's website. Many researchers and policymakers have referenced and used this research in their academic work and policy making, respectively.

While in Rwanda, I found time to volunteer as a tutor of undergraduate economics and mathematics courses at the University of Kigali. During that time, I also had the opportunity to visit landmark sites, such as the Kigali Genocide Memorial Center, for a sober moment and remembrance of the 1994 Rwandan Genocide. I concluded my overseas research trip with an excursion to the Virunga National Parks to see the different chimpanzees and gorillas.

As for a high school student, you do not need to wait to be a college student, graduate student, or career researcher for your research to be credible and make a strong impact in the world. There are numerous cases where high school students made discoveries that advanced and contributed to the civilization of humankind. Many times, discoveries and new ideas are accidental and out-of-curiosity exercises. At other times, the findings result from the quest to solve an existing problem. For instance, if your interest is in the area of STEM, you could discover a new idea that not only adds to the body of literature, but also changes people's lives. It is even more impactful if you discover a new idea that has a practical use in a developing country in Africa, Latin America, and Asia, where many local problems need local solutions. Out of many discoveries, here are two examples made by high school students for your inspiration.

Deeply concerned about the lack of clean drinking water and electricity for many people in developing countries, an Australian student, Cynthia Sin Nga Lam, successfully invented a cheap portable device called H2Pro that provides purified water and generates electricity. She achieved this by conducting research combined with her class knowledge of the chemical process called photocatalysis, which uses light. Her invention was one of the finalists in the Google Science Fair in 2014.

Another high school student, Remya Jose, from India, was troubled by the exhausting way people in her town hand-washed cloth

Cynthia is sitting next to her H2Pro, water purification device. Steffen, A. (2019). *Teenager Invents Two-In-One Device That Generates Electricity And Purifies Water* [Photograph]. Intelligent Living. https://www.intelligentliving.co/teenager-invents-two-in-one-device-generates-electricity-purifies-water/

using water from the nearby river. To ease their suffering, she decided to invent a pedal-powered washing machine. Through encouragement by her teachers, she used scrap bicycle parts and some engineering skills to design a machine that neatly washes clothes, saves water, and uses no electricity. The pedaling takes a few minutes, which are good exercise moments, to completely wash the load.

Remya on her pedal-powered washing machine.
Rodriguez, O. (2016). *14-Year-Old Girl Invents Pedal-Powered Washing Machine From Bike Parts* [Photograph]. Habitat. https://inhabitat.com/14-year-old-girl-invents-pedal-powered-washing-machine-from-bike-parts/

IV. Faculty-Led Tour and Study

This is a coursework-related tour or study led by a faculty member to any country of choice. A high school teacher can also lead this kind of tour. It is mainly offered during a school holiday. Though most tours are credit-based, some are only for excursion and expedition purposes. The primary purpose of the faculty-led tour or teacher-led tour is to reinforce class lessons through visual experience and experiments. If you are offered this opportunity, especially one that takes you back to your country or continent of origin, you should take advantage of it. It is unlikely you will find time to volunteer on the side but the trip will offer a wealth of experience, perspective, and lessons that may launch your future plan.

Overseas Career-Related Activities for College and High School Students

I. Common Volunteering Programs

The central message of this book is how to leverage your available resources and time as a student and youth to contribute to the country and continent of your origin as well as humanity at large. The word "cause" in the subtitle of this book is all about volunteering and making an impact. There are boundless and inexpensive opportunities to volunteer as a student and youth. Here are some options.

A typical diaspora family takes a vacation to a country of origin now and then to reunite with relatives, connect, and introduce children to the family members. This vacation is often during long holidays when schools are off for about one to three months. As a student, this is an ideal opportunity to do something productive that will impact your future and serve an underprivileged community in the country of origin. Besides making your plan to enjoy a family vacation, you should also plan a time to volunteer during this trip.

What if your family holiday does not coincide with the time you plan to volunteer? In this case, if you are at an age allowed by international travel, you can simply plan your trip primarily for volunteering purposes but also as an opportunity for vacation. If you go to the country of origin, it is recommended to stay with a reliable relative in that area if you need to save money, connect, and improve language skills.

As for funding your trip, there are few ways. If your parents are able to, they can sponsor your trip. Otherwise, if you have savings from holiday work, this will be a worthy cause for which to use it. You can also check with your local community leadership if they will sponsor trips of this kind. Another option is to do online fundraising through a platform such as GoFundMe. As a last resort, if you have a source of income and do not have enough cash at that moment, you could borrow from a friend, bank, or even your parents.

Whether traveling with a family or alone, you need to have a concrete volunteer plan beforehand. Decide if you want to volunteer in a career-related field that reinforces your skills or any area that serves some of the most disadvantaged groups, a cause for humanity. If you are traveling alone and prefer to use an international volunteer program, there are many reliable organizations to choose from. Global Leadership Adventure (GLA), Volunteering Solutions (VolSol), and Plan My Gap Year (PMGY) are great fee-based volunteering organizations. If you are looking for a non-fee based program, there is Peace Corps, Doctors Without Borders, or other similar organizations. However, they may be inflexible in terms of location and work preference. For more specific information on a choice of organization and volunteering work type, here are a few common ones.

Volunteering in a School

As a student, you are often freshly equipped with knowledge and skills from class. This provides you with an opportunity to teach and tutor students at a lower academic level that befits your skill and interest level. For instance, a college student with good grades and skills in STEM courses can teach or tutor at any high school level. A competent high school student can teach at any elementary school level, also known as primary school in many countries.

It is even more impactful if you can teach in an area that impart life-changing skills to underprivileged students. For example, if you are fortunate to teach in a school with a computer lab and internet, you can arrange for coding, programming, or robotic software to be installed into the computers, and introduce the students to these valuable skills. After you leave, some self-starter students can teach themselves and achieve excellent results. Alternatively, if the school has a science lab, you can teach or tutor students with science lessons and practicals. In the absence of these facilities, you can teach mathematics or English.

As a student from a country with a robust education system, in many instances you are more trained and skilled than many teachers who are teaching those students, especially in STEM subjects. Therefore, before you embark on the vacation trip, start by researching a disadvantaged neighborhood, slum, and town schools close to where your family will be staying. If you plan to travel alone, do research first on the location where you will live and the school where you would like to volunteer. Your starting point should be non-profit organizations (NPOs) and non-governmental organizations (NGOs) on the ground. In particular, most countries have education non-profits actively recruiting volunteers to help in their facilities and schools they support. You can contact their information representative and they will likely point you to the right person. If you prefer to work with the school directly, you can call up the school administration to check if they can take you as a volunteer tutor or a co-teacher. As mentioned earlier, the chances are high that they will give you the offer if you can provide verification through grades and references. If you have education materials to donate, let the representative know ahead of time, as that may give them more motivation.

Volunteering in a Hospital and Health Institution

A great ancient Roman poet, Virgil, once said, "The greatest wealth is health." That is, if one is not healthy, one cannot be productive at a given task. Life simply becomes difficult. For this reason, health care should be a universal right. Yet, quality health services are not accessible to most people in the least developing countries. Healthcare professionals, like nurses, medical doctors, psychiatrists, surgeons, pharmacists, healthcare administrators, and dentists just to mention a few, are inadequate in most of these countries. The situation is even more dire in African countries where there is one doctor for more than 1,000 people. According to the U.N., factors such as lack of adequate training institutions and resources, brain-drain, and the pay gap are to blame for the shortage.

If you are a student in a medical field, you can volunteer in your country of origin or any other developing country. By doing this, you can gain a rewarding experience and knowledge out of this challenging situation. For instance, if you are a nursing student volunteering in a rural clinic with an overwhelming number of patients and only one doctor, you can be assigned to the roles of a medical doctor, such as diagnosing and prescribing medications. If you happen to be in one of the southern hemisphere countries, the skills and experience you can get by working with patients suffering from tropical diseases may be unique and vital for your career. Common tropical diseases, such as malaria, yellow fever, cholera, dengue, and yellow fever are primarily found in Latin American, Sub-Saharan African, and some South Asian countries. Likewise, neglected tropical diseases (NTDs) like leprosy, hookworm, Buruli ulcer, and many others are mainly confined to the southern hemisphere regions. As a student in a medical field from a western country, you will not get this first-hand experience at any university in the West. Your experience here could inform your future research and other potential career endeavors.

If you are a young healthcare professional taking time off to volunteer, your service will go a long way in saving lives and making an enormous impact on the community you will serve. It will also be an opportunity to enhance your career perspective and add an impactful paragraph to your resume. To find the hospital you would like to volunteer in, check the ministry and department of health website and ask the representative for information on government and private hospitals and health facilities. Also, international and local health NGOs and NPOs tend to have answers for volunteers on their websites.

Volunteering in an Orphanage

Every country has orphanages that come into being due to children who lost parents, lack of means to support children, neglect, and abandonment. These factors are multiplied in worn-torn and poor developing countries, hence, creating a flood of orphan children. If there is not proper care given to orphan children, many may die, and some become street children and criminals. In order to manage these social risks, government agencies, NGOs, and NPOs set up orphanages to care for orphans from infants to teenagers. The orphanages give a range of care including social activities, school learning, physical services, emotional support, and overall health services.

The challenge is that many orphanages often lack adequate resources to do their tasks. Some of the enormous challenges with which orphanages have to deal are deficient workforce, poorly constructed and maintained facilities, and funding shortages. As a diaspora orphanage volunteer, you have a handful of choices. Whether you teach them in class, take them to the playground every day or do their household chores, anything helps in providing a warm care environment for the orphans.

Supporting Sports

As a young person, you may have a love of one sport or two. You may be a star of your school team. You may have a plan to make a career out of it. All of which is great. Apart from several significant health benefits, playing a sport builds your leadership skills, self-confidence, and new connections. If you reside in a developed world, chances are you are having fun and smoothly sailing through with your sport activities and aspirations.

However, in other parts of the world, there are many youths who want to play for fun or aspire to become professional sport players, but do not have the basic needs to play the game. Things like sport clothing and uniforms, shoes, and even the balls are rare privileges for most youths in disadvantaged communities. Thus, these children get creative, improvising footballs, also known as soccer balls, by blowing air into balloons and wrapping them with thick clothes.

If you are a young diaspora person, who loves sports, and would like to share the love of the game and put a smile on children's faces somewhere in the world, you can do something. To witness your impact in person, you can mobilize sporting materials and travel with them to a place of your choosing, in a city slum neighborhood, a refugee camp, a displaced camp, or a rural town. Despite the challenges and harsh environments, there is much raw talent in these places. You never know, you could be supporting the next LeBron James or Lionel Messi of the world.

Here are two inspiring stories of people who took action in this area. First, is a South Sudanese-Australian football star, Awer Mabil, who plays in Europe. In 2014, while visiting Kakuma refugee camp, Awer and his brother, Awer Bul, carried 20 balls with them to distribute to the refugee boys. Upon seeing massive demand for the balls, Awer and his brother returned to Australia and started a non-profit organization called Barefoot to Boots, which provides sporting and other essential needs to refugees in Kakuma and beyond.

On the national level, an exemplary example is a South Sudanese-British NBA player, Luol Deng, who retired from the NBA in 2019 and made another career move to help the South Sudan National

Basketball team. In the same year he retired from the NBA, Luol Deng accepted to run as the president of the South Sudan Basketball Federation and was unanimously elected. He took the position not for monetary compensation, but as a national duty. After 15 grueling seasons in the NBA, Luol could have easily opted to enjoy his retirement in any Western country, but instead decided to return home to move South Sudan's basketball team forward. And he did. In 2022, after three short years, the South Sudan Basketball team went from a relegated ranking to number 76th in the FIBA World Ranking and 11th in Africa. This made it the team with the highest improvement in the shortest time possible. Luol achieved this by giving it his best through coaching, motivation, and even paying for some of the team expenses out of his own pocket.

Other Important Volunteer Programs

The volunteer programs mentioned above are just a few of many programs. However, there are other equally important ones, such as wildlife and environmental conservation programs, gender-based violence (GBC) initiatives, street-kid projects, disabled people initiatives, and child care programs. The key is to choose one based on your interest and the impact you want to make.

II. Invention Project

If you are gifted with mechanical or technological skills, you can support needy communities with an invention project. There are a host of problems and challenges in underdeveloped countries, varying from lack of basic needs, such as clean water, food, and shelter, to lack of basic services, such as electricity, education, sanitation, and healthcare. Your invention could solve one of these problems and change poor people's lives. There are many cases where young people, out of ingenuity combined with some class knowledge, have come up with remarkable inventions that have transformed many people's lives. Besides changing lives, there is a high chance you could develop intellectual property around your invention vision and commercialize it for a wider use. For your motivation, here are three examples.

In a poor rural Malawian village lived a boy named William Kamkwamba. While in high school, he had to drop out because his family could not afford to pay his school fees due to a famine that hit his region. In 2001, disturbed by his family's circumstances, he decided to put his intellectual curiosity about "energy" into action.

William inspects his wind turbine invention.

Haq, Z. (2021). *William Kamkwamba, the African Youth Who Seizes the Wind [photograph]. Green Network.* https://greennetwork.asia/figure/william-kamkwamba-the-african-youth-who-seizes-the-wind/

In one of his local library visits, he found a book called *Using Energy* that explains how to harness and use energy. Using metal junkyard materials, bicycle pieces, and tree parts, he invented a wind turbine that powers electrical devices, such as a phone, radio, and light bulb. This was a significant relief to his family and many people in his village. Energized by the enormous impact of his first invention, William went on to invent another windmill for irrigation.

After unveiling his first invention, the international media picked up the story, and William became an instant celebrity. He got invited by various shows to talk about his invention and future projects and plans. One of these plans was the book titled, *The Boy Who Harnessed the Wind,* he co-authored in 2009. The book became required reading for freshmen at several universities in the U.S. and beyond. On the top of that, his invention was made into a documentary film, *William and the Windmill,* which won an award for the Best Documentary Feature in 2013 at the South By Southwest Film Festival. Subsequently, the book was developed into a film, *The Boy Who Harnessed the Wind,* in 2019.

On the technological side, a former war child, Lual Mayen from South Sudan, is making an impact out of his experience. Lual was born in a displaced person camp (IDP) of Aswa, then Sudan, and later moved to a refugee camp in northern Uganda. He grew up in a survival environment, often lacking the bare minimum of basic needs. Nevertheless, determined to change his life and the world, he meticulously followed his passion for computer science. Due to his incessant requests as a teenager, his mother struggled and scraped for a few years and bought him a laptop. With a few tutorial resources

Lual shows his video game, Salam.
Vaughn, E. (2019). A Kid In A Refugee Camp Thought Video
Games Fell From Heaven. Now He Makes Them. [Photograph].
National Public Radio (NPR). https://www.npr.org/sections/
goatsandsoda/2019/12/11/786740227/a-kid-in-a-refugee-camp-
thought-video-games-fell-from-heaven-now-he-makes-them

from a friend, he taught himself coding and programming skills.

While still in high school, he developed an interest in making video games. The quest led him to the United States where he realized his full potential. Thinking about how to make an impact as a video game developer, he started a company, Junub Games, with its first game, *Salam*, launched in 2019 at the Games Awards. When it premiered, it was watched by over 26 million people worldwide.

The name of the video game, *Salam*, an Arabic word for peace, says it all. His goal is to advocate for peace and promote conflict resolution among the people in war zones and inoculate virtual game players with compassion for the victims of wars. Built into the game, the empathy is generated when a game player places themself as a refugee running away from air bombardments. To prevent the character from dying, the player has to buy, with real world money, water and food for the character. A portion of this money goes to humanitarian organizations to help the refugees and IDPs around the world.

The last item on the invention project topic is on a light that scares away the predators. A few years ago, Richard Turere, a boy from the Masaai tribe of Kenya, was bothered by lions that regularly killed his village livestock at night. He decided to make a device dubbed as the Lion Lights. For Richard, this project started at 11 years old as a hobby of disassembling and assembling electronic equipment. Then when the right time came to put his skill set into use, he took it as a responsibility to save his village livestock from lions and other predators.

After learning that lions are frightened by flashing lights, he gathered an old car battery, a solar panel, a flashlight, a light switch, and a motorcycle indicator box to make a device that flashes around the clock at night. The Lion Lights not only chase away lions but also scare off leopards, cheetahs, and other carnivores.

With the support of the NGOs operating in the area, Richard has successfully installed nearly 1,000 Lion Lights in homes in his village. As a positive side effect, his invention has managed to reduce revenge killing of the lions by the Masaai warriors, hence alleviating the potential

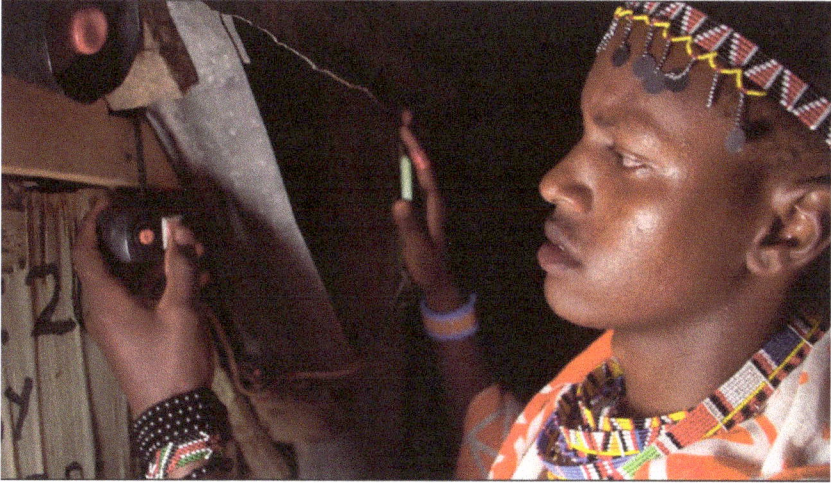

Richard demonstrates with the Switch.

Crellin, O. (2018). What happened to the boy who chased away the lions? [Photograph]. British Broadcasting Corporation (BBC). https://www.bbc.com/news/business-44398952

endangerment of the lions. Due to its effectiveness, his device has spread and is now used in other countries such as India and Argentina.

In conclusion, William and Richard accomplished their invention with less resources, using scrap materials, and less academic knowledge. If you are an aspiring diaspora engineering student who wants to make an impact, you have more knowledge and resources at your disposal. As for the source of funding, your local diaspora community could fund your initial project, if you have a potential impactful invention. Alternatively, just like Lual, you could leverage your technology skills to make changes in your homeland and the developing world in the area of your interest.

III. Technical and Vocational Education and Training (TVET)

The importance of TVET was officially launched and recognized in Seoul, South Korea on April 30th, 1999 at the United Nations Educational, Scientific, and Cultural Organization (UNESCO) Conference. Broadly, UNESCO defines TVET as "aspects of the educational process involving, in addition to general education, the study of technologies and related sciences, and the acquisition of practical skills, attitudes, understanding and knowledge relating to occupations in various sectors of economic and social life."

The importance of TVET cannot be overstated. The mechanics, electricians, technologists, masons, nurses, agriculturalists, and other technical and vocational workers, very much run an economy. Hence, a substantial part of economic growth and stability rests with the productivity of these workers. The other remarkable contribution of TVET is the promotion of social equity in many countries. Marginalized youths, women, disabled people, and people from less privileged backgrounds are often locked out from acquiring education and life-changing work skills from traditional learning institutions. However, with the push and popularization of TVET, governments have been able to provide TVET for free or at a minimal cost to these groups. Private sector TVET institutions have also filled the gap in areas with high demands. In aggregate, this has increased employment opportunities and boosted socio-economic advancement in developing countries.

There are several TVET models around the world. Some countries have integrated TVET into primary and secondary education. Other countries use it as an alternative to the traditional college education.

Still other countries operate TVET as stand-alone work learning institutions. To enhance its effectiveness, UNESCO recommends the integration of TVET into secondary and tertiary education.

If you are endowed with TVET skills, you have many opportunities to contribute and impart your skills and knowledge in person to other young people through TVET institutions in developing countries. As mentioned in the previous paragraph, depending on each country's TVET design, you can volunteer in a primary, secondary, vocational, or technical school. Programs such as computer programming and coding, graphic design, computer networking, computer information system, and many other technical programs often demand volunteers at TVET centers. If interested, contact the school administrator in charge of a program. A simple online search can also lead you to the right person.

IV. Youth Leadership Academy

A youth leadership academy provides programs to develop and enhance leadership skills in young people seen as potential future leaders. An academy gives these youth tools and skills to solve some of the world's most pressing issues such as the sustainable development goals (SDGs). The skills can either be in business, NGO, or political leadership. Business leadership includes tools and skills around entrepreneurship and innovative businesses. Political leadership training provides skills on good governance and oratory competency capable of rallying masses around a given cause. Through this leadership training, the potential young leaders improve their self-confidence, self-esteem, and networking as part of the end goals.

There are many youth leadership academies for different types of work that include but not limited to sport, music, finance, and police work. As the theme of this book, the focus is on the leadership academy that particularly promotes socio-economic advancement. An excellent example is the African Leadership Academy (ALA) School in Johannesburg, South Africa. ALA was co-founded in 2004 by Stanford University graduate, and one of the Time Magazine's 100 Influential People in 2019, Fred Swaniker, to develop the next generation of leaders who will propel the continent's growth. The academy is a pro-Pan Africanist school that admits exceptional students from Africa and around the world, who have the drive to solve the continent's seemingly intractable development issues.

ALA offers programs such as a two-year Diploma, Global Scholars Program, Model African Union, Africa Careers Network, and BUILD-in-a-Box. Among these programs, Global Scholars Program (GSP), a short-summer program, is best suited for most diaspora students. GSP accepts promising young leaders between 13 and 19 years to learn about impact-related ventures through practical lessons, interaction with influential entrepreneurial leaders, and continent exploration. On financial aid, ALA provides support only to those in need. For more information, visit the African Leadership Academy's website.

V. Internship

In today's age of globalization, you may not know for certain where your future job will be located. Even if your job starts in the country of your residence, the same company may transfer you to another country, or your second job could be in an overseas developing country. For this reason, if you are a college or graduate student, it does not matter where you do an internship as long as it is with the same intended company or organization. Fortunately, due to economic globalization, many multinational corporations are now offering internships in all of the locations where they operate. In nearly every sector, there are multinational enterprises operating in every continent. For example, British Petroleum (BP), Google, and JP Morgan, among others, are operating in many developing countries. Besides corporations, numerous overseas internship opportunities are also available through United Nation (UN) agencies, NGOs, and NPOs.

As for a high school student, there are also many overseas internships available for your education level. You can search for companies that offer internships to high school students. If you do not know where to start, you are better off using an internship placement provider if you can afford it. An internship placement provider, also called a program provider, is an organization that matches you with an internship opportunity of your choice. Their fee level determines the number of services they provide, and hence is correlated with the chance of securing an internship. The fee goes to pay for services such as internship search, housing, food, visa processing assistance, guidance, and other administrative support. Furthermore, if you want to get college credit for your internship, some program providers liaise with universities and companies to make it happen.

An internship can either be paid or unpaid. Other than the pay or stipend, the benefits of both paid and unpaid internships are exactly the same. But since internship opportunities in high skill-based sectors can be very competitive, and even rare, many young people forgo the internship pay in the hope of making it up in the future. Additionally, you can choose a traditional office setting or virtual internship depending on your needs and interests.

Taking an internship comes with many advantages. In both developed and developing countries, there can be more skilled people than jobs in some industries, such as IT job seekers in India. In other countries, the population is growing faster than available jobs. However, in other countries, the major problem is the lack of skilled people to do certain talent-based and technical jobs, whether as an employee or a self-employed person. This is the reason companies often complain about the lack of "qualified" people to do particular jobs. This is a common problem in both underdeveloped and developed countries. Thus, doing an internship while still a student plays a critical role in boosting your career skills. Besides giving you an edge in a job application, an internship helps in building your network that you can use in the future for all kinds of benefits. If you are a high school student, doing an internship can give you an advantage in your college applications, as this suggests to the admission officer that you are a self-starter, a hard worker, and an ambitious person.

As a recurring theme of this book, if your internship is not directly related to work impacting an underprivileged community, you can find time to volunteer on the side, if possible. This can be one of your marks in making a change in the world. Also, if you happen to be in a country of origin, this would be a great chance to connect with kin and kith before heading back to your country of residency.

Trip Preparations

Once you know the neighborhood where you will stay in and the location where you will volunteer, it is essential to make other key preparations, especially if you are traveling alone for the first time. Visit your doctor to get tropical medicines for diseases such as malaria, cholera, and yellow fever. Make sure you have travel health insurance, and if possible, you can add extra travel coverage. More importantly, maintain a few contact numbers overseas and back home for emergencies. Lastly, check and have valid travel documents and requirements ahead of your travel date. Certainly, this is not an exhaustive list.

Benefits of Participating in an Overseas Volunteering Activity

Most schools around the world encourage their students to have international exposure. According to Harvard University, "Over half of Harvard College students participate in an international experience during their time as an undergraduate." Apart from the personal experience and career enrichment mentioned throughout this chapter, there are several institutional benefits you garner by participating in overseas academic and non-academic volunteer programs. Once you successfully complete a volunteer program, the school, hospital, or organization may provide you with a letter of appreciation, general letter recommendation, and academic and language credit documents. They can also be your reference source for any future college or job application.

Risks Associated with Overseas Volunteering and Study Activities

Although traveling overseas for vacation, volunteering, and study can be fun, rewarding, and enriching experience, there can be risks associated with your trip. In most cases, the chance of any risk materializing while traveling is not more than in your country of residence, as any event can happen anywhere in the world. However, being a new arrival in a particular country can expose you to some risks since you are unfamiliar with the laws and environment. Therefore, the key is to take cautionary and preventive measures that reduce or eliminate the chance of any event from happening. Here are some of the main risks and ways to keep yourself safe.

Sickness

When you travel, you hope to enjoy your trip without any hindrance. Nevertheless, the longer you stay in a place, the higher the possibility of getting sick especially from common ills. For instance, if you are in a southern hemisphere country, malaria is prevalent in certain seasons due to mosquito bites. Also, if you are away from your family and friends for the first time, you may experience homesickness, which could lead to stress and even depression. In this case, if necessary, call home to talk with your parents and friends. If possible, join social clubs to meet and make new friends. Overall, in case of a serious sickness, seek professional medical services at the nearest reputable medical facility that takes international health insurance coverage. If you need urgent care, and the hospital doesn't take your health insurance, you may pay out of pocket and get reimbursed later by the health insurance. Contact your health insurance for this option and other recommended requirements, such as extra covered items, before leaving for the trip.

Terrorism and Civil Violence

In the recent decades, acts of terrorism have become a global concern. In developing countries, there were incidents of terrorist groups hitting big cities, such as Nairobi, Dar es Salam, Mumbai, and others. In Western countries, there has been a rise in terrorism as seen by glaring images in New York, London, Paris, and Christchurch. On the other hand, cases of civil violence emanate from rebel groups fighting governments, and aggrieved groups such as citizens protesting a certain cause. To avoid such risks, gather as much information as you can. Get tourist and visitor information from the concerned government department of the country you are visiting. Your resident country's department or ministry of foreign of affairs should also have traveler information for the country you are visiting. If you travel through an organization and institution, they will have an orientation or a guidance session before starting your work or study. Also, you may ask a relative, friend, or peer who has knowledge of the place you are visiting. Overall, the chance is that you will not avoid traveling to a country due to prior terrorism and civil violent incidents or existing threats. This is where the guidance and safety information prepare you for the hotspots to avoid.

Accident

An accident can happen for any reason, including but not limited to tripping, swimming, and playing game. This section emphasizes accidents resulting from transportation vehicles and other machines being commonplace in the modern era. The probability of getting into this kind of accident increases if you are in a new place where you are unaware of driving and general safety rules. Fortunately, you can minimize or eliminate the possibility of getting into an accident if you follow this advice. Avoid driving when in a country you are unfamiliar with the driving rules and regulations, especially for a short trip of a few weeks. If you are on an exchange program or a volunteer work mission, some schools and organizations have vehicles for shoppings and outings. If you are staying with relatives, have a reliable and legal driver from the family drive you around. If you are staying in a hotel, they may have a driver that takes customers around. If the hotel does not have a customer car, the front desk staff should be able to recommend a particular taxi company that takes their customers to places.

Transgression

It is a beautiful world out there, and everyone should explore and contribute to it one way or the other without fear. However, while on a vacation or good cause mission, unpleasant event may happen. This can be in the form of a crime like theft, sexual harassment, discrimination, verbal, or physical abuse.

Often, when you are in a new country for the first time, the local residents can tell that you are a foreigner, whether by your skin color or simply by how you walk and talk. Unfortunately, some bad actors may exploit this unfamiliarity.

To protect yourself and your properties, the key is to be in the right place, at the right time, with the right person. This entails avoiding unfamiliar neighborhoods, dark alleys, and corners. If you are a female, avoid walking alone outside your home at night at all costs.

Leave valuable materials you do not need at home. Other issues that may cause harassment and discrimination are that particular country's cultural and social values. Many countries have specific norms and rules on dressing style, alcohol and drug use, political and religious expressions, and same sex relationships. For location-specific risks, ask a relative, peer, or friend who possesses such information. If your trip is through an organization and institution, refer to their informational brochure, website link, and concerned staff for particular information.

PART II

Distant Support Activities and Programs

Chapter 3

Volunteering Without Traveling

"Volunteers do not necessarily have the time; they just have the heart."

— American Author, Elizabeth Andrew

C hanging the world comes in different forms and shapes. Certainly, traveling overseas and seeing in person the impact—all those smiles and happiness—you bring to someone's life is exhilarating. However, the impact you make while at the other side of the ocean is equally important, especially if your circumstances do not allow you to travel. Whether your hurdle is a school, job commitment, lack of resources, or whatever the circumstance, there are several other ways to support causes in your country of origin and any other country while staying in your country of residence.

I. School Supplies
Stationery and Books

Saying we live in an unequal world is an understatement. In affluent societies, mundane things like pens, pencils, and notebooks are taken for granted by students. In other parts of the world, such as in a village or slum school, a typical student does not get sufficient school stationery. In this case, students are forced to save notebooks for more important lessons and home works and memorize other lessons when necessary. In the worst case, especially for first graders, students are made to use their fingers as pens and the ground as writing papers.

For these poor village students, owning curriculum books for study is a privilege. Having curriculum books is a preserve of the teacher, who uses them to prepare lessons. But even then, many teachers do not possess the curriculum books due to their lack of means. Some lucky pupils whose parents struggled to buy them books end up sharing them with other siblings, cousins, and friends, hence further reducing their studying time. Yet, these schools typically do not have libraries where students can do supplementary and general readings.

Your support can go straight to these students in different ways. First, identify a school you would like to support. Pick the country, county and district, and the particular school through research, connection, or prior knowledge. Suppose you and your friends manage to mobilize a significant amount of stationery. In that case, you can reach out to an international NGO or NPO operating in that country which can ship them for free or at minimum cost.

Through follow-up communications with concerned individuals, you can track the shipment from the shipping point to the point of distribution to the intended beneficiaries. Despite their network challenges, the school staff in charge should be able to send you and your peers the pictures and videos of the distribution of stationery. The school staff can do this by visiting a location with a better network or cyber cafe. This process is important for accountability and transparency purposes.

The second option is to mobilize stationery and books and donate them to a trustworthy education charity operating in that particular location. This option relieves you the hassles and stress of tracking the shipment to the intended recipients. To assure where your donation went and what it has done, some charities will send you a thank you letter with pictures and videos of the school and students impacted by your generosity.

The third option is to find a reliable individual or organization on the ground near the school you would like to support. Give them the money with specific details of stationery and books you want them to purchase and the name of the beneficiary school. The advantage of this option is that the books will be for the local curriculum, whether for the library or individual student's use. As a positive side effect, your purchase will add to the stimulation of the local economy.

STEM Resources

In the 21st century, you may be surprised to hear that most students in sub-Saharan Africa and other least developed countries do not have access to STEM resources and facilities. According to UNICEF, "less than 1 in 20 school-age children from low-income countries have internet connection at home, compared with nearly 9 in 10 from high-income countries." The deficiency weighs more heavily on public than private schools.

As a diaspora student and youth who would like to support a school in need with STEM resources, you can organize your technology equipment, such as computers, ipads, and tablets, and send them directly to a computer lab at the school in need or for students' possession. If you prefer an organization to facilitate your project, you can donate your electronic equipment to an established education NPO or NGO operating in the area of your choice.

Supplying science lab materials is also highly recommended. Science lab materials may not be readily usable if the school of your choice does not have a facility or trained teachers. However, you can donate lab materials to a school with a science facility but lacking adequate resources. Alternatively, you can avoid the challenges of overseas transport by purchasing a number of newly-invented science lab device called the Science Set.

Science Set is essentially a science lab packed into a portable device. Science Set was invented by a Ghanian entrepreneur, Charles Ofori Antipem, and approved and lauded by the African Union (AU) as one of the top innovative solutions to STEM education challenges. The set holds more than 45 materials and at least 26 science experiments for primary and secondary school levels. The device is affordable, easy to store, and ready for use with minimal training time.

A student uses the Science Set for Experiment.
Source: In Ghana, pocket-size labs turn more children to studying science, by C. Antipem, 2019, Global Partnership for Education (https://www. globalpartnership.org/blog ghana-pocket-size-labs-turn-more-children- studying-science). Copyright 2019 by Dext Technology/GPE

II. Scholarship and Tuition

Tens of millions of children worldwide are out of school due to conflict, cultural practices, diseases, and poverty. A staggering number of these children left school or never were in school due to poverty. The majority of these children are in Africa, Latin America, and South Asia. This is directly reflected in the slow development of these regions.

Nelson Mandela once said, "Education is the most powerful weapon which you can use to change the world." In essence, he means, through education, a son of a poor farmer can become the engineer that devises the innovative technique to build a country's highways; a daughter of a charcoal burner can become the doctor that finds the vaccine for malaria; a son of a blacksmith can become the president that takes his country from one of the poorest countries to an advanced country. A child you support today with education could be any of those pioneers tomorrow.

Sponsoring a poor child's education needs through scholarship and tuition payment is the best way to affect this change. Depending on the country's cost of education, and whether the school is boarding or day, public or private school, about $1500 can sponsor the four years of a child's secondary school education needs. Depending on the number of years of sponsorship, the cost may be lower for a primary school education. You could do this with two other friends, by providing $ 500 each. If you skip a few of your enjoyments and extravagances such as concert tickets, an extra pair of shoes that you do not need, and some party nights, you can save the money for this purpose. Alternatively, if you have holiday job earnings, you can quickly raise your share from it. That is a cause bigger than yourself.

How do you go about searching for a child in need? You can contact a random village primary school in the country of your choice and find out that bright child who could not continue to a secondary school or dropped out before completing primary education due to the lack of school fees. You can also contact a scholarship charity in the location of your interest to give you a student that you can sponsor. If you would like to support the other million refugees and internally displaced children, you can donate to UNICEF, Save the Children, and other international education organizations.

III. Virtual Teaching, Tutoring, and Peer Mentoring

In this digital age, you can practically accomplish many things from the comfort of your couch, saving time and money you might not have. Although the internet network may be poor in most rural areas and small towns, numerous students live and study in towns and cities with a good network. However, they go to schools with no well-trained teachers and proper learning facilities.

One of the best ways to support these underprivileged students is through virtual tutoring, teaching, and mentoring. If you have very good grades in subjects like mathematics, English, and sciences, you can readily find a school and student needing a virtual tutor and teacher. You can teach or tutor those students below your academic level. For instance, if you are a senior high school student, you can tutor a junior, sophomore, freshman, or a primary school student. On the other hand, if you are a college student, you can teach or tutor at any high school level. Additionally, a mentor provides and boosts a mentee with hope and aspirations for the future. As an academic peer mentor, your job is to look for and recommend opportunities for your student. Discussing and recommending opportunities on international scholarships, college applications, sports, research, internships, and foreign exchanges are great ways to help the mentees. Overall, for accountability purposes, the beneficiary school's representative may verify your background through your transcripts and references. For information on how to get hold of a student in need, reach out to the schools, education NPOs, and education authorities in the location of your interest.

IV. Telemedicine and Telehealth

Lack of access to healthcare services is a great cause of suffering, poor health, and deaths among many people in countries with inadequate healthcare systems. This is a pervasive problem in rural areas of underdeveloped countries. It also affects poor city dwellers who cannot afford necessary hospital visits. In the process, people for whom earlier disease detection and screening would have prevented death may not benefit.

With the advent of telemedicine, a diaspora health professionals such as a doctor, nurse, radiologist, and clinician can volunteer remotely. A health professional can offer services, such as prescription, diagnosis, and patient monitoring, on a phone or a video call. For example, a medical professional can seek to provide service through a government health department that delivers medicine by drones to rural clinics but lack adequate doctors and nurses. A health professional can also offer a range of preventive health and administration services, such as mental health counseling, data keeping training, and other services from the comfort of their office to any underserved clinic in the world.

Providing these distant health services can alleviate the problem of poorly trained and lack of qualified specialists. It is also a very efficient way to volunteer for those who do not have the time or resources to travel longer distances. For the patients, their ills may be prevented and cured, with their overall health outcome improved and longevity increased. This in turn leads to better productivity levels that strengthen a personal and national economy.

V. Volunteering For an Organization

The diaspora people living in developed countries have government registered Community-Based Organizations (CBOs) and Non-Profit Organizations (NPOs) that serve their members in their countries of residence and people in their homelands. A CBO can be made of members of a certain ethnic, regional, cultural, or religious group who fundraise and contribute membership funds for the organization's operation. A CBO offers a range of services such as sponsorship of a community event, church space, tuition, and scholarship. In addition, a CBO can also support humanitarian causes in the homeland of its members. On the other hand, there are small NPOs run by individual members that serve the members of that particular community in their country of residence, and others serve the people in their country of origin. If you prefer to volunteer in this kind of organization, you can seek a position on the leadership team or as a regular volunteer.

Non-Governmental Organizations (NGOs), such as World Vision, Oxfam, Save the Children, Doctors without Borders, and many others are bigger international organizations which provide all kinds of humanitarian services. On a similar range, there are United Nations (UN) Agencies, such as UNICEF, UNHCR, UNDP, and others, which are intergovernmental organizations that promote peace among nations and provide relief to refugees and internally displaced persons of its member states. All these organizations are always looking for volunteers to support their mission and operations. By volunteering for these organizations, you are also indirectly supporting the people in your country of origin and humanity as a

Meeting with the African students at UC Berkeley, October 2018. Some of the students became volunteers for South Sudan STEM Initiative.

whole. For more information on volunteering, visit the nearest branch location or the organization's website.

Benefits of Distant Volunteering

The advantages of distant and overseas volunteering activities are the same, except for the overseas traveling experiences. While you may miss out on exciting overseas experiences, you can still garner other crucial benefits such as career enrichment and academic enhancement from volunteering at a distance. If you volunteer for an organization or volunteer as an individual, you can use it in your future school application and job resume. Some organizations provide appreciation and recommendation letters. This could give you an edge over other applicants.

Chapter 4

Investment in the Country and Continent of Origin

"I believe that we have reached a stage in life in the economic development of Africa where moving forward is perilous, moving backwards is cowardice and standing still is suicidal but we must persevere because winners do not quit and quitters never win."

- A prominent professor of
Law and Pan-Africanist,
PLO Lumumba

The previous sections looked at channels you can contribute and make an impact to your community, country and continent of origin, and the world without expecting a return. This section explores how you can achieve the same goal and objective with an expectation of a profit through investment. Responsible and ethical investment promotes economic growth and job creation, hence reducing poverty.

I write this section with an understanding that most students and youths do not have necessary funds for investment purposes. However, it is important that this information is provided for those with capital and future plans. For those with investment plans, the first questions that may come to your mind are business risks-related. What return will I get out of this business? How safe is this investment? How secure is this investment destination? These are a few of many questions that a diligent potential investor should ask.

In particular, investing in developing countries can be more risky than investing in developed countries with established institutions, rule of law, and infrastructure. In developing countries, the main risks are weak property rights, lack of physical and technological infrastructure, lack of strong consumer base, and political and economic risks. However, the ultimate investment losses can happen even in the safest places. For starters, in 1992, a hedge fund manager, George Soros, bet against the British Pound, and he won, leading to the increase of his hedge fund value by more than three billion dollars. This led to the depreciation of the British pound and subsequent rise in prices of goods and services and a loss of value of investment assets in the U.K. In September 11, 2001, terrorists attacked the Twin Towers in New York City, which resulted in immense loss of wealth among the investors and untold human suffering. Then there was the Great Recession that started as a result of over-leveraging in the housing market in the U.S. in late 2007. The Great Recession spread from the housing market into financial markets around the world and culminated in the loss of tens of trillions of dollars. The point is that risk exists in every investment and country.

The key is to have a solid vision and strategy for due diligence on risk factors in each sector and industry of the country of your investment. Read the government investment policies and legal guidance paperwork as every country has unique requirements. Visit or call the concerned ministry and department staff to inquire about your concerns. Make connections and discuss with other investors in the industry. In fact, being a diaspora investor gives you two distinct investing advantages. If you have your dual citizenship documents, you can invest as a citizen of your country of origin with full rights, privileges, and benefits of a citizen. Conversely, if you do not have a dual citizenship status, as it is not allowed by some countries, you could invest as a foreign citizen through a scheme called foreign direct investment (FDI), which has its own benefits and privileges. The following are the foremost sectors that are central to economic growth and alleviation of poverty in developing countries.

Agriculture

1.1 Farming Industry

Farming is the most essential industry through which most people make a subsistence living in emerging and underdeveloped countries. Many countries, especially in sub-Saharan Africa, South Asia, and South and Central America, have vast virgin fertile land that is unutilized for commercial-scale and export-oriented production. At the same time, a rapid population growth in developing countries combined with prevalent natural disasters, such as drought, famine, and flood, has increased global demand for food. This makes commercial farming a lucrative business enterprise. As a local producer, with a minimum transport and labor cost, you can achieve a very high return.

Whether an individual or a group establishes a firm, the benefits to local people and the country can be enormous. Not only can it lead to increase in food production, but it can also give rise to vast employment opportunities. For instance, if a firm embarks on agricultural production and agro-processing, most of the workers, including at the senior level will likely be drawn from a local labor force. Besides being employed, the employees can also benefit from higher wages. In this case, the permeating effect of your investment can be a remarkable employment benefit, which can result in the reduction of the national poverty rate.

1.2 Animal Husbandry and Related Industries

On the livestock front, many countries in the developing world are endowed with these resources but with a minimum contribution to growth and poverty reduction objectives. For example, the Food and Agricultural Organization (FAO) concludes that, "South Sudan is one of the richest countries in livestock wealth per capita in Africa, boasting more than 40 million livestock: 12 million cattle, 12.1 million sheep and 12.4 million goats." Although the pastoralists own most of this livestock, it can generate an incredible amount of wealth if they are encouraged and incentivized to invest much of their wealth into the commercial sector.

An aspiring investor can seek partnership with local or international investors to start a business, such as a ranch, slaughterhouse, cannery, tannery, or dairy product firm. Fortunately, it is common to find local entrepreneurs on the ground seeking partnership with outside investors as this can bring significant capital investment, expertise, and technical knowledge to their enterprise. Meanwhile, the government agency in charge should help to oversee, regulate, and promote products locally, regionally, and globally. In the end, this can create a significant number of employment and growth opportunities.

Physical Infrastructure

These are buildings, roads and bridges, sewage, drainage systems, and other infrastructural features of a country. One of the key reasons countries do not thrive as they should is the lack of physical infrastructure, such as transportation networks, that facilitates economic activities such as trade. The African Union (AU) finds "Intra-African trade stands at around 13% compared to approximately 60%, 40%, 30% intra-regional trade that has been achieved by Europe, North America and ASEAN respectively."

An excellent example of a diaspora investment in physical infrastructure is as follows. In 2016, a group of 45 Lost Boys, who live in the U.S. and Australia, decided to pull together funds, with each contributing a few thousand dollars annually. With the funds, they formed an organization called Centerpiece Global Partners Limited, headed by Gabriel Maketh Kuer, to manage the project. In just four-and-a-half years, they bought land and built 28 beautiful upscale homes at the outskirts of Nakuru City, Kenya.

Photo Credit: Centerpiece Global Partners Limited.

Khor, M. (2021). Not Long Ago, We Started From an Empty Plot, but Three Years Later, We Have This Peaceful Neighborhood. [Photograph]. Centerpiece Global Partners Limited. Facebook Posting, by Maketh Kuer Khor, on May 27, 2021.

During and after the completion of the project, many indirect and direct jobs were created; that is, from common laborers to engineers and managers were hired locally, not to mention hundreds of thousands of dollars directly added to the Kenyan economy through purchase of local materials.

Per capita electricity generation, 2021

This is annual average electricity generation per person, measured in kilowatt-hours.

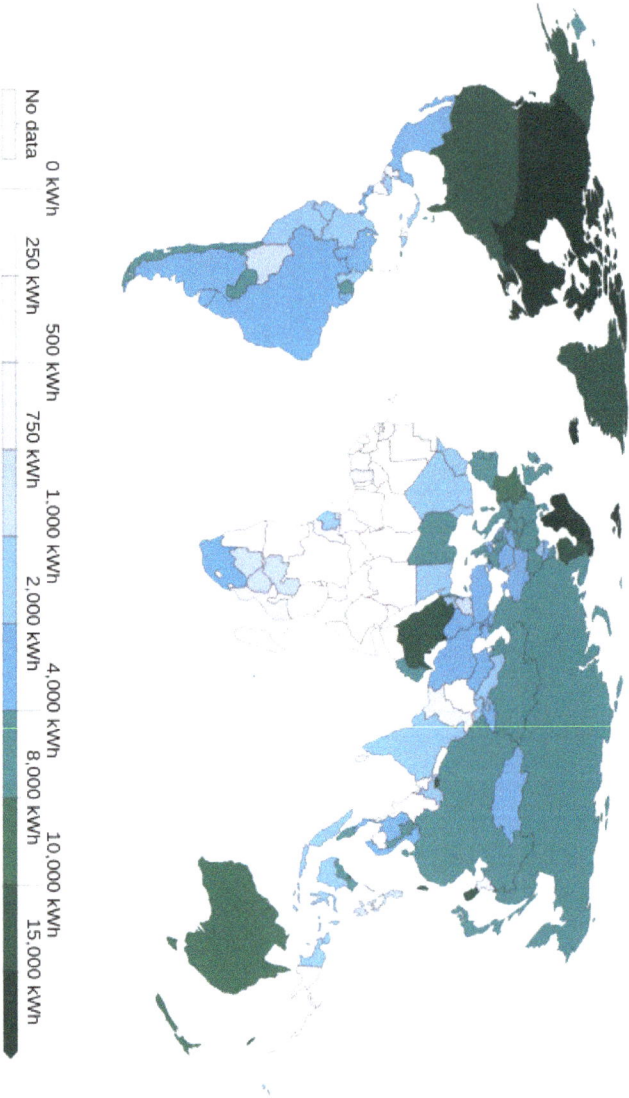

| No data | 0 kWh | 250 kWh | 500 kWh | 750 kWh | 1,000 kWh | 2,000 kWh | 4,000 kWh | 8,000 kWh | 10,000 kWh | 15,000 kWh |

Our World
in Data

Energy

Energy is a critical ingredient of development. Having adequate and sustainable sources of electricity can lead to strong economic growth and prosperity. In the opposite figure, it is apparent that sub-Saharan Africa lags behind most of the world.

An entrepreneur and investor should see opportunities in these challenges. Higher growth and return opportunities are stronger in undeveloped and emerging markets from an economic perspective. Economists call this free entry. In other words, there is minimal competition in this sector in developing countries whereas developed countries may have saturated markets in this sector. Therefore, diaspora members can play an important role through investment in the energy sector of their countries and continents of origin. Whether your investment is small or large scale, it adds to the aggregate effect on development.

Here is a remarkable example of a diaspora investment in electricity. In 2014, a Senegalese-American singer, Akon, and two others started a solar energy initiative, Akon Lighting Africa, to bring affordable clean power to rural towns and cities across Africa. The enterprise encourages solar energy for street lighting, businesses, and home use. Within a few years, Akon Lighting Africa, managed to bring solar energy to millions of people and employed several thousand people in 18 African countries. This also means having power at night leads to increases in productivity and economic growth, thus a poverty reduction.

Information and Communication Technology (ICT)

An ICT sector in a given economy comprises data centers, hardware enterprises, software enterprises, and all related communication components essential for personal, business, and government use. An adequate ICT sector facilitates transactions and increases work productivity. Some experts tout growth in global technology use as a miracle which will leapfrog least developed countries to the developed stage in the shortest possible time. They cite many indigenous technological innovations such as mobile banking platforms like M-pesa, where M stands for mobile and pesa is a Swahili word for money, in Kenya. They also point to the prevalent use of dual sim cards in Africa, Indonesia, India, and other developing countries and the faster growth of bandwidth usage in underdeveloped countries.

Despite these improvements, several billion people worldwide still have no access to the internet. This structural deficiency was exposed by COVID-19 pandemic that had far more devastation in low-income and middle-income countries than in rich countries. In low-income and middle-income countries, most people did not have the privilege to work at home to avoid contact with other infected people. Even as the governments ordered COVID-19 lockdowns, most people in developing countries could not work at home due to the lack of ICT infrastructure and training. This led to an increase in poverty and several social problems, such as school dropout. This retarded the social progress of these societies as more children dropped out of school due to teenage pregnancy, forced marriage, lack of school fees, and child labor.

If you are a potential creative entrepreneur, the financial return can be high in these largely untapped ICT markets in low-income countries. Areas such as telemedicine, biotechnologies of cattle diseases and rustling, farming technologies, rural internet access resources, and many others can be lucrative ventures. You could simultaneously maximize your return and benefits to the local community and country through job creation and service opportunities. Fortunately, synergies are also being created as cheap renewable energy like solar power becomes more accessible.

Education

Many current developing countries have a low enrollment problem of school-age children. Yet for socio-economic transformation to happen, there is a need for a universal primary education. Nevertheless, the major problem lies in what happened at the end of the education pipeline. Does a typical high school or college graduate get a job shortly after graduation? If so, does that job make them earn a comfortable and sustainable income? Overall, the answers to these questions vary dismally depending on the country. To put it differently, the education quality of the graduates is more important than the quantity being graduated.

Historically, during the Western industrialization era, from the late 18th century to the early 20th century, the workers ranged from having no formal education to basic education. The industrialists have to train the workers with necessary skills to accomplish various tasks. With recent industrialization, particularly in the East Asia region, education has been upgraded to include tertiary level but with a greater focus on formal STEM and TVET education. This model has enabled the fastest development pace in the history of humankind, as it lends itself in a productive manufacturing and technology export-driven growth. A prime example in this case is a group of East Asian countries popularly named as Asian Tigers, a metaphor for the fastest development speed. Asian Tigers comprises Singapore, Hong Kong, Taiwan, and South Korea. They went from being in the category of the least developed countries in the 1960s to developed world status in the 1990s. A miraculous feat accomplished in just one generation.

Today developing countries still require a development model and strategy similar to that of the Asian Tigers but customized to suit local conditions and realities. This can be done. It is in the works in Rwanda, Botswana, India, among others. Politics aside, let us take Rwanda, as an example. After being pillaged and plundered during the 1994 Genocide, Rwanda rose remarkably from the ashes. Under President Paul Kagame, the government has instituted development-focused reforms since the early 2000s. Being less endowed with natural resources, the country seeks a knowledge-based economy as the source of growth. To make this happen, the government started with education reforms focusing on STEM education at their 6-3-3-4 traditional educational system, with alternative options for a TVET certificate at upper secondary school level and polytechnic degree at tertiary level. Despite other existing developmental challenges, these reforms have produced impressive results for the country. Rwanda has become one of the few developing countries to have achieved the UN Millennium Development Goals (MDGs) on universal education and health coverage. The country has also become one of Africa's top foreign direct investment (FDI) destinations. Together, these reforms have lifted at least a million people out of poverty, about eight percent of the country's population.

Suppose you are a prospective impact-oriented investor in the education sector. In that case, you can target and put your funds in the kind of education that produces marketable and technical skills of the future. One highly recommended area is to invest in a primary and secondary education. For example, if you or your group have adequate funds, you can build a private secondary or primary school and then equip the school with adequate learning facilities, such as a science lab, computer lab, and library. Alternatively, you can go for a TVET secondary school. For tertiary education, opening a polytechnic school can significantly impact that country.

As many graduates come out of school equipped with technical and vocational skills, it creates a more productive labor force. It also furnishes the labor market with hard skills, therefore encouraging the inflow of FDI. Simultaneously, a new generation of innovative entrepreneurs can crop up that further create more jobs and economic growth, thereby contributing to the country's overall welfare.

Other Important Sectors

The aforementioned sectors are commonly found in all countries through a shared control by private enterprises and governments. However, other sectors are equally important but may be designed differently to fit a country's development strategy. A country may tailor these other sectors based on government industrialization policy, natural resource endowment, available human capital, and technology access. These sectors include industrial, healthcare, financial, natural resource, utility, and tourism and hospitality.

In particular, you may have an investment limitation in these sectors for the following reasons. Some governments may have a monopoly or partial control of the industry through state-owned enterprises. A country may not have a natural resource endowment essential for your business. A county may not have a readily available human capital and technology infrastructure for your business. Thus, you may need to explore and research extensively each of these other sectors before investing.

Conclusion on Overseas Volunteering, Distant Volunteering, and Impact-Oriented Investment

If you are a diaspora student or youth who is thinking of a channel to support the country and continent of your origin or any developing country, this book gives you various options or may reinforce your ongoing plan. In Chapter II, the book gives you options for a student and youth's overseas academic, volunteering, and career-related activities. Also, while on a non-volunteering activity, the chapter explores how you can volunteer along the side. Chapter III provides ways to support various causes while staying in your country of residence. Chapter IV examines an option for an impact-oriented investment in any of the various sectors. That is, getting a financial return while making an impact in a community and country.

If you are a young diaspora person whose parents or grandparents migrated from another country, you may have heard many tragic and good stories. Your father might have suffered as a soldier. Due to war, your mother might have gone through adversities as a young girl. Your parents might have migrated to your present country due to political and economic upheavals or religious oppression in their country of birth. These were the struggles of your parents' generation. As a young diaspora person who is still connected to the country of your origin, whether you will go back and reside there or not, you have a role to play in any way that can advance its socio-economic progress. This is the fight of your generation. And in any generational cause, everyone is expected to contribute in one way or the other. This is what this book is all about.

Essentially, the book is like one of your favorite restaurant menus. In the menu, there are descriptions of all the foods which are serve. Some of which you crave, and some not so much. Every time you visit this restaurant, you cannot miss out on eating one of your food choices. In the same way, the country of your origin is like one of your favorite restaurants, where you can choose from the list of impact-making activities, menu descriptions, as a way to support it.

Chapter 5

Notes to Parents

"The solution to adult problems tomorrow depend, in large measure, on how children grow up today."

- Prominent American Anthropologist,
Margaret Mead

Book Summary

The book started with my background as one of the Lost Boys of Sudan. At about seven years, I was one of the youngest boys when the journey started. For starters, the journey of the Lost Boys of Sudan was a tragic one necessitated by the civil war in Sudan. The boys escaped from their ancestral villages and walked hundreds of miles to Ethiopia. A few years later, they were forced out by the civil war in Ethiopia back to Southern Sudan and onto Kakuma refugee camp, Kenya. In the early 2000s, they were resettled in various cities in the U.S. as refugees. I started the book with my background to inspire young people. When a young person, in particular a diaspora one, reads what the Lost Boys went through, I hope that young person will say, "I am lucky I didn't go through that," and will no longer take their life for granted.

In Chapter 2, I introduced the theme of the generational cause and sense of purpose. In particular, a diaspora student or youth from a developing country is encouraged to play a role in supporting a cause that impacts disadvantaged people in their country and continent of origin. The subsequent sections provided detailed channels through which a student or youth can support causes in their country of origin or any other country. Overseas academic programs such as study abroad, exchange study, faculty led tour, and research programs were discussed. Traveling overseas for career-related programs and volunteering activities were also explored. Many of these programs are fully or partially funded, depending on each school or company. While overseas on any of these programs, a student is encouraged to find time to volunteer on the side.

Chapter 3 provided volunteering options that a young diaspora person can participate in without traveling overseas. This option, called volunteering without traveling, is necessary knowing some constraints and challenges may prevent a student and youth from traveling overseas. Chapter 4 provided a choice for impact-oriented investment, for those youth with investment plans. To help with an investment decision, this section takes the potential investor through various challenges and opportunities of investing in a developing country. This was done through the analysis of each economic sector.

The book's key theme is its ability to weave volunteering and impact-oriented goals into academic, career, and investment activities. This purposely incentivizes and motivates the participant to take action. Hence, the subtitle, "The Cause That Matters in Your Curriculum, Career, and Connection," the three Cs of the book. As a parent, you should finish reading this chapter at the minimum. To effectively guide your child on any of these programs, I highly recommend you read the whole book when your time allows. This way, with better understanding of the context, you can share ideas with your child.

Is Your Child at a Crossroads?

A typical first-generation parent considers themself a diaspora person. They have that urge and the longing to return to their homeland someday. A study by an international policy research organization, STATT, cited by Australian Broadcasting Corporation (ABC) in 2012, indicates 90% of the first generation of South Sudanese-Australians hope to return home in the future, temporarily or permanently. However, this percentage drastically decreases with any diaspora group's second, third, and subsequent generation.

The main focus of this book are the children of the first-generation parents, whether the children were born overseas or in their current country of residency. A diaspora parent would like to see their child connect to their country of origin. The connection to the land of origin can take different forms. It can be participating in activities that promote progress, such as a volunteering program, an investment enterprise, or a diaspora political program. It can mean visiting, moving and resettling back temporarily or permanently. The former is the subject of this discussion. If a young person can get connected to the aforementioned activities and programs that in the future may in itself induce their moving back or regular visits to the country of origin. At the minimum, as an adult, it will make them stay interested and connected in perpetuity to the country of origin. The question is, how do you get to this point as a parent? Firstly, let us delineate existing risks and challenges in the context of the diaspora people. Following this, potential solutions and opportunities for a young diaspora person and their parents will be proposed.

Problems, Risks, and Challenges While Raising a Child

Perhaps you have an obedient child, a promising child with no social problems. Then all you need is the continued guidance and nudging along the direction you would like them to take. At the other end of the spectrum, many parents struggle to control and raise their children in responsible ways. In several Western countries, it is widely known that many African and Latin immigrant young men, on average, have problems integrating into their respective countries of residence. Many feel suspicious of the societies they live in and manifest identity crises by isolating and making friendship with those that look like themselves. They have a higher incarceration rate and felony charges than their white counterparts. They are involved in various serious crimes and vices such as alcohol abuse, robbery, homicide, drug dealing and use, and thuggery. On the other hand, many young immigrant women of color have their share and set of common crimes and vices, like physical fighting, shoplifting, drinking, dropping out of school, negative peer pressure, and teenage pregnancy. Most of these crimes and vices are the result of various factors, such as poor parenting, family instability, socio-economic factors, unfair policing practices, and a host of other variables beyond the scope of this book.

Potential Solutions and Opportunities for a Child at Risk

The key to avoid a child deviating from social norms is the early identification of risks and signs. Once you do this, you could reduce a child's time and space and occupy it with more productive things. As the saying goes, "An idle mind is a devil's workshop." Giving a child too much free time and space can lead them to explore and experiment with negative things. The subject of this book is the positive thing that a young person can engage in during their free time. An action that gives them a sense of purpose. A cause that gives them hope and sense of belonging. A situation that humbles them and builds their empathy. One worthy cause that can fill up this free time is volunteering. There are numerous impactful volunteering opportunities for your child. There are several activities they can do while sitting in their room, such as virtual teaching, tutoring,

Former U.S. President, Barack Obama, with his
grandmother, Sarah Obama, in Kenya's Kisumu area.
[Photograph of Barack Obama's step-grandmother Sarah passes away in Kenya at
99]. (2021). https://www.newindianexpress.com/world/2021/mar/29/barack-
obamas-step-grandmother-sarah-passes-away-in-kenya-at-99-2283202.html

and mentoring other peers in any part of the world. At the diaspora
community level, they can participate in the local youth engagement
and empowerment programs, such as being part of the community
youth leadership and fundraising. When taking an overseas family
vacation, you can reserve some time for your child to volunteer at a
local school, hospital, orphanage, or charity organization. Taking a
family vacation in the country of your origin with your child may

have a lasting impact on their behavioral change when you return to your country of residency. The moment your family arrives in your homeland, you will be ceremoniously welcome, especially if it has been a very long time apart. In some cultures, the child may be lifted and carried on the shoulders by cheering relatives as a sign of happy welcoming. Other cultures do traditional dances, ululating, and singing around the child and the family. When the child speaks, people may cheer even if they say only a few words in the local language. This welcoming and show of affection activities can be very powerful when a child internalizes it as a sense of belonging. Having also seen the challenges in their ancestral land, the child is unlikely to take their opportunities and privileges for granted when they return to the country of residency.

On the language side, while on an overseas family vacation, make your child spend a lot of time around new friends, cousins, and relatives. They will quickly pick up and improve their speaking ability, even if it is just for a few weeks. When the child reaches the age allowed by international travel, they can arrange their own trip to spend more time with the family and have more time to practice speaking the language. Linguistic experts recommend this as one of the best methods to improve language speaking skills. It is very important that the child speaks your language to allow them to connect with your people, roots, and culture. A perfect example is the Jewish diaspora group which has thousands of schools around the world that teach Jewish culture and language to their children. Besides schools, they encourage every young Jew in the diaspora to visit the State of Israel. As the result of these engagements, the vast majority of the Jewish diaspora's children speak and/or write Hebrew. For more programs and activities that positively engage a child refer to Chapters 2, 3, and 4 of this book.

Source of Funds for an Overseas Activity and Program

There are several opportunities that a student can leverage to secure the funding for an overseas academic, volunteering, and career-related activities. These sources of funds have not been taken advantage of by many diaspora students. They are unexploited resources. Many high schools, universities, and volunteering organizations offer scholarships, grants, and loans for foreign exchange, study abroad, and research activities. The overseas program can be partially or fully covered, depending on the school.

Admittedly, many Western high schools and colleges may not have academic partnership programs with counterpart schools in developing countries and may not offer financial support. In this case, it is incumbent upon a parent to financially support a child interested in an overseas academic, volunteering, and career related program. For example, your child may have savings, from a holiday work, that they want to use for a flight ticket and accommodation but short on funds for other necessities. Besides their academic project, if the child wants to volunteer at a school, they may need to go to the facility with supplies like stationery and books to donate to the students. If the child wants to volunteer at an orphanage, they may need some clothes and toys to donate. Your child may ask for some funds to cover the cost of these items, among others.

Benefits of Youth and Student Overseas Programs to a Parent

The advantages of impact-oriented programs and activities to a student or youth have been discussed at length in the previous chapters. If your child has read the book, they are likely aware of those personal benefits. What has not been discussed is how these activities and programs benefit the parent in the long-run? Typically, a diaspora parent's largest investment is in their child. But for a parent who likes their child to have roots in both their countries of residency and origin, they may get frustrated that their child doesn't want to learn about their country of origin. A parent might say "my child" just wants to be American, Australian, Canadian, or other nationalities. The child might tell a parent, "I do not care about your country of origin, I was not born there." In the process, a parent may lose hope in trying to teach a child about their ancestral background. Do not lose hope. Former U.K. Prime Minister, William Churchill once said, "The pessimist sees difficulty in every opportunity. The optimist sees opportunity in every difficulty." This book refutes the assertion that a typical child born in the diaspora cannot have affinity to their ancestral roots. The child can embrace both roots. You could be a proud parent by taking some of the prescribed actions narrated in this book. Your child could be a CEO of that impactful global company. The child could become an inventor of a device that changes the lives of millions of people. The child could be one of the most influential figures in the world. Great examples are Barack Obama, Luol Deng, Dikembe Mutombo, R&B Singer Akon, and others who have changed the world and their countries of origin in their own ways.

If you are a diaspora parent who plans to retire in your country of origin, you would certainly like to have your adult child regularly go and visit you in the future. Depending on the circumstance, your adult child could even move back together with you, thus making it easier to see each other. This can make your retirement more enjoyable. There is no better way to build this affinity than making your child hooked on your country of origin while still a teenager. Additionally, several studies have confirmed a significant positive correlation between a child-parent relationship and longevity. That is, the stronger the social ties and understanding between a parent and child, the longer the parent is expected to live. The social connections come in the forms of an elder parent taking on advising roles, spending fun times with an adult child, and playing a grandparent role.

Benefits of Overseas Youth and Student Programs to the Country of Origin

Sometimes, a parent may underestimate the potential and change their child can bring to the world. This is the essence of having a child get interested in volunteering for a good cause to bring forth their talent. A gifted and creative young person can save many people from dying in a given country. Through their impactful inventions, like some of those mentioned in the previous chapters, the child can save needy people of the world. That is changing the world. Consequentially, once the child sees the impact of their first invention, it is more likely that they will become a serial innovator of ideas, thus becoming one of the global shakers and shapers.

While many studies indicate that the diaspora groups are not significant for the growth of the developed countries of Europe and North America, the diaspora groups are crucial for developing countries' socio-economic progress. The diaspora communities bring the much needed development resources to their home countries in form of brain gain, foreign direct investment (FDI), domestic investment, and remittances. These resources have been critical in the development processes of countries, such as Ethiopia, India, Egypt, Kenya, and many others.

References

Websites

25 million children out of school in conflict zones. (2017, April 24). UNICEF. https://www.unicef.org/ press-releases/25-million-children-out-school-conflict-zones

African Union. (n.d). *BIAT–Boosting Intra-African Trade.* Retrieved June 7, 2022, from https://au.int/en/ti/biat/about

FAO Livestock Show and Agricultural Exhibition to promote food security. (2020, January 14). FAO. https://www.fao.org/ south-sudan/news/detail-events/en/c/1258579/

Harvard University. (n.d). *Study Abroad.* Retrieved June 7, 2022, from https://cabot.harvard.edu/study-abroad

Ighobor, K. (2017, March). *Diagnosing Africa's Medical Brain*

Drain: Higher wages and modern facilities are magnets for Africa's health workers. United Nations. (https://www.un.org/africarenewal/magazine/december-2016-march-2017/diagnosing-africa%E2%80%99s-medical-brain-drain

Kerin, L. (2012, November 26).*90pc of Sudanese refugees want to go home* - https://www.abc.net.au/news/2012-11-26/90pc-of-sudanese-migrants-want-to-return-home/4392956

Two thirds of the world's school-age children have no internet access at home. (2020, November 30). UNICEF. https://www.unicef.org/press-releases/two-thirds-worlds-school-age-children-have-no-internet-access-home-new-unicef-itu

University of Adelaide. (n.d.). *Study overseas as part of your University of Adelaide degree.* Retrieved June 7, 2022, From https://www.adelaide.edu.au/study-overseas/#why-should-i-study-overseas

Vocational education and training (VET). (1984). United Nations Educational, Scientific and Cultural Organization (UNESCO). https://unevoc.unesco.org/home/TVETipedia+Glossary/filt=all/id=545

Thesis

Mayom, D. A. (2015). *The Impact of Foreign Direct Investment on Labor Market Measures: Evidence from Sub-Saharan Africa* [Master's thesis, University of San Francisco]. Institutional Repository at the University of San Francisco. https://repository.usfca.edu/thes/144/

Images

Antipem, C. (2019). *In Ghana, pocket-size labs turn more children to studying science* [Photograph]. Global Partnership for Education. https://www.globalpartnership.org/blog/ghana-pocket-size-labs-turn-more-children-studying-science

Crellin, O. (2018). *What happened to the boy who chased away the lions?* [Photograph]. British Broadcasting Corporation (BBC). https://www.bbc.com/news/business-44398952

Haq, Z. (2021). *William Kamkwamba, the African Youth Who Seizes the Wind [photograph]. Green Network*. https://greennetwork.asia/figure/william-kamkwamba-the-african-youth-who-seizes-the-wind/

[Photograph of Barack Obama's step-grandmother Sarah passes away in Kenya at 99]. (2021). https://www.newindianexpress.com/world/2021/mar/29/barack-obamas-step-grandmother-sarah-passes-away-in-kenya-at-99-2283202.html

Rodriguez, O. (2016). *14-Year-Old Girl Invents Pedal-Powered Washing Machine From Bike Parts* [Photograph]. Habitat. https://inhabitat.com/14-year-old-girl-invents-pedal-powered-washing-machine-from-bike-parts/

Steffen, A. (2019). *Teenager Invents Two-In-One Device That Generates Electricity And Purifies Water* [Photograph]. Intelligent Living. https://www.intelligentliving.co/teenager-invents-two-in-one-device-generates-electricity-purifies-water/

Vaughn, E. (2019). *A Kid In A Refugee Camp Thought Video Games Fell From Heaven. Now He Makes Them.* [Photograph]. National

Public Radio (NPR). https://www.npr.org/sections/goatsandso-da/2019/12/11/786740227/a-kid-in-a-refugee-camp-thought-video-games-fell-from-heaven-now-he-makes-them

www.ingramcontent.com/pod-product-compliance
Lightning Source LLC
Chambersburg PA
CBHW041300040426
42334CB00028BA/3096